MANAGING INTERGROUP CONFLICT IN INDUSTRY

Managing

Intergrou

PREPARED FOR: THE FOUNDATION
FOR RESEARCH ON
HUMAN BEHAVIOR
ANN ARBOR, MICH.

Conflict in Industry

ROBERT R. BLAKE, PH. D.
Scientific Methods, Inc., Austin, Texas

HERBERT A. SHEPARD, PH. D.
Case Institute of Technology, Cleveland

JANE S. MOUTON, PH. D.
Scientific Methods, Inc., Austin, Texas

GULF PUBLISHING COMPANY
HOUSTON, TEXAS

MANAGING INTERGROUP CONFLICT IN INDUSTRY

First printing December, 1964
Second printing July, 1966
Third printing February, 1968

Library of Congress Catalog Card Number 64-8696

DEDICATED TO

CAROLYN AND MUZAFER SHERIF

Preface

Knowledgeable managers of today are aware that there is useful knowledge scattered through the behavioral science literature. Most of them also believe that closer contact and better communication between managers and behavioral scientists help to make behavioral research more useful in their organizations. But they are often frustrated because existing knowledge is too seldom organized and focused in a way to be useful to them in solving their own organizational problems.

Behavioral scientists who have worked with real-life organizational problems also recognize the difficulties of applying available knowledge. The successful solutions to these problems do not often fit neatly to the highly specific findings coming from the specialized fields of behavioral research. With rare exceptions, behavioral scientists who provide consulting, training or research services to organizations find that they must have and be able to use a wide range of knowledge and skills if they are to be truly helpful. Their effectiveness in helping to design and implement programs of organizational improvement depends on their knowledge and wisdom in the use of findings in various areas such as interpersonal and group dynamics, leadership, motivation, communication and organization theory.

The authors of this book were faced with a choice of audiences. The management of intergroup conflict in organizations is an area of obvious practical importance, but it is also one in which the relevant behavioral research findings are scattered throughout the specialized literature of several professional disciplines, and not too well known by most behavioral scientists. A book written primarily for other behavioral scientists would be timely. It would review in detail the contributions from a variety of research sources, providing the original data where possible, and of course focus on the theoretical questions involved. Such a book would be a further contribution to behavioral research literature, but it would not be usable to managers of large-scale organizations.

Instead, the authors decided that they would write primarily for the many potential users of behavioral knowledge about intergroup conflict and its management, the managers themselves. While the traditional caveat that "more research is needed" still applies, there is an adequate basis of knowledge about intergroup conflict from which to derive useful guidelines to staff and line managers, labor leaders, and others who have intergroup conflicts to resolve. Therefore, this book is a blending of behavioral knowledge with guidelines to innovative practice in intergroup conflict management. As such, it is not likely to interest behavioral scientists as much as managers.

Since this book is an integration of existing research and theory (without the traditional technical vocabulary or footnotes), it is important to note how the authors have organized it. There is an underlying model or way of looking at conflict in terms of three basic dimensions, which is both original and integrative. Moreover, the presentation is straightforward, beginning with the delineation of the model and moving from primitive to more sophisticated solutions—from the win-lose trap to problem-solving. Managers will find a clear statement of the proposed guidelines to action.

The professional qualifications of Professors Blake, Shepard and Mouton in the field of psychology are too well known to need amplification. What may not be so well recognized is that they have for many years combined academic teaching and behavioral research with extensive personal experience as consultants and trainers in programs of organizational improvement in industry. Thus the book makes full use both of their professional training and experience as behavioral scientists and also of their wide experience in practical application of behavioral knowledge.

The Foundation for Research on Human Behavior is pleased to have a part in an effort such as this, an effort to make significant behavioral knowledge more useful to business and related organizations. Indeed, the understanding of conflict which this book provides may not be limited in its application to business or labor organizations. It may have useful implications for conflict in the family, the school and the community, and eventually even for national and international affairs.

Hollis W. Peter
President
Foundation for Research
on Human Behavior

ANN ARBOR, MICHIGAN
OCTOBER, 1964

Contents

Foundations and Dynamics of Intergroup Behavior

This book covers matters of vital significance in managing conflict in industry. It deals with achieving effective coordination between units of an organization, such as management and union, sales and operations, staff and line, headquarters and field.

The behavior of two members of a corporation in relation to each other is determined by three or more sets of forces. The first of these is formal job description—the kinds of responsibilities each brings to the situation. That is, each routinely behaves according to the requirements of his role within the corporation. Secondly, their behavior is determined by their backgrounds of training and experience. A case in point is a foreman who has risen from the ranks, discussing an issue with a graduate engineer. The third factor which determines their behavior is the role they feel themselves to be in as representatives of a particular group in the corporation. For example, in a discussion between the Vice President of sales and the Vice President of manufacturing, each may be representing a viewpoint arrived at and held with conviction by himself and other members of his group.

Our major focus of interest in the following chapters is on the third set of complex forces, but, for clarification, the first two are discussed briefly. Intergroup relationship problems are dealt with thereafter.

BEHAVIOR AT THE INTERPERSONAL LEVEL

When a man speaks as a group representative, his behavior is to some extent dictated by the fact that he is a member of that group. In contrast, when a man speaks from the framework of his job responsibilities, he speaks only for himself. In the latter case, disagreement between the parties is a *personal* matter.

Factors Influencing Supervisory-Subordinate Relations Where Disagreement is a Personal Matter

Industrial organizations usually have a number of mechanisms for resolving interpersonal disagreements. For example, when a subordinate disagrees with a supervisor on a job-related issue, the supervisor can resolve the difference in several different ways. The supervisor may decide to resolve the matter himself; he may turn it over to his subordinate; or he may "table" the matter. Alternatively, the supervisor may seek a third position to which they both can agree. In any event, the procedure for resolving the conflict and the ultimate decision lies with the supervisor.

Resolving Interpersonal Conflict Between Peers

In most respects, a similar situation exists where individuals are peers rather than supervisor and subordinate. They may be unable to satisfactorily resolve their differences through argumentation. Finally, when each is unable to influence the other and an impasse is reached, they can take the matter to a common supervisor. The supervisor can then dispose of the matter through his higher authority. However, the complexity of a conflict situation increases greatly when the disagreeing parties are representatives of different groups, as will be discussed shortly.

The point of these illustrations is to show that where individuals are acting in their own behalf, or simply within their job responsibilities, they normally are able to resolve their differences with relative ease. Resolution may be accomplished through argumentation, by administrative action, or by the introduction of additional facts.

FACTORS INFLUENCING THE RESOLUTION OF A DISPUTE WHEN DISAGREEMENT IS AN INTERGROUP MATTER

Though superficially similar to the two-person relationship examples, significant differences appear when a person's interactions with another are dictated by his membership in or leadership of a group. Under these conditions, *the individual is not free* in the same sense as the person who acts independently out of job description or rank alone. Now the person's behavior is determined by many additional factors.[1]

The Dynamics of Group Interplay in Resolution of Disputes

In situations where an individual is interacting with another and both are representatives of groups, additional forces, quite complex, come into play. Acting as an individual, a man is free to change his mind on the basis of new evidence. But as a group representative, if he changes his thinking or position from that of his group's and capitulates to an outside point of view, *he is likely to be perceived by them as a traitor.*[2] On the other hand, if as a representative, he is able to persuade a representative of the other group to capitulate to his point of view, *his group receives him as a hero*. In other words, when a man is acting as a representative of one group in disagreement with another, the problem is no longer a personal affair. It is an *intergroup* problem. And as such, it can become a significant factor in accounting for his actions—as we will see.

Group Responsibilities of Individual Members

Often, men are quite aware that they have responsibilities as group representatives as well as individual job responsibilities. But formal organizational practices and attitudes often prevent this awareness from being discussed or from being openly considered.

As an example, consider the situation where the Vice President of sales speaks with the Vice President of operations. Formal organizational theory commonly assumes that each man speaks for himself, out of the background of his individual job and responsibilities. In practice, however, each may be keenly aware that he is representing the goals, values and convictions of his own group, and furthermore, when he speaks for them, he also speaks for himself. When problems between sales and operations seem difficult to resolve, it is not, as a rule, a sign of rigidity, incompetence, or personality conflict.[3] Rather, it is more likely to be a product of the complex task of seeking resolutions which will not violate the attitudes, values, and interests of the many other persons that each represents.

Incompatible Group Norms, Goals and Values

Just as formal organizational theory, as written, recognizes only that the individual speaks for himself out of his job responsibilities, similarly it may fail to recognize other facts of organizational life. Formal organization theory assumes that the goals, norms and procedures of different functional groups in the organization are, by definition, similar, complementary or identical. The Vice President of sales and the Vice President of manufacturing are aware that their groups are similar and thus complement each other. However, they are also aware of wide differences and disparities in the viewpoints and goals that may exist between the groups they represent. As mentioned, if the interactions of these men were based entirely on job description, and a disagreement were to arise, there would be adequate organizational mechanisms for dealing with it. Similarly, if men only dealt with one another out of clearly agreed-upon concepts of organization purpose and procedures, there would be little room for disagreement and dispute.

There is increasing recognition, however, that neither of these circumstances accurately describes many situations in modern industrial life. This recognition has led to an acknowledgment that men, in fact, are group representatives within the framework of an organization. In turn, it has led to an awareness and appreciation of how an individual acting as a member, or as a leader, of a group, is confronted with a host of additional problems.[4] These problems must be dealt with in terms of their genuine complexities if unity of organizational purpose is to be achieved.

The roots of these complex problems which group representatives face are characteristic of groups and of individuals. As will be seen, group membership is complicated further by the characteristics of intergroup relations. After looking briefly at these characteristics of groups, we will turn our attention to the dynamics of intergroup relations.

THE STRUCTURE AND PROCESS OF GROUPS-IN-ISOLATION

There are a number of ways of describing the characteristics of groups-in-isolation which we should consider prior to dealing with industrial intergroup relations.[5, 6]

Regulation of the Interdependent Behavior of Members of Groups-in-Isolation

Fundamentally, a group consists of a number of individuals bound to each other in some stage or degree of interdependence or shared "stake." Their problem is to guarantee the survival of the group in order to attain some *purpose or goal.* Taking for granted that the group's goals are clearly understood by its members, the interdependence among individuals, then, must be regulated to insure partial or entire achievement of these goals.

The Emergence of Group Structure, Leadership and Normative Rules

The need to regulate interdependence leads to three further properties of groups. When these properties emerge in group life they become additional forces which influence individual behavior. Let us look at each of these.

1.   *Group Structure.* A differentiation of individual roles often is needed to accomplish group objectives. Differentiation inevitably results in some individuals who have varying degrees of power to influence the actions of others. The result is that some group members carry greater weight than others in determining the direction of group action, its norms, values and attitudes.

2.   *Leadership.* When the power system among members of an informal group is crystallized, it is common to speak of *that individual with the most power as the leader.* In some groups, he is boss, or supervisor; other members are subordinates. The leader is looked to by the members for guidance and direction. The power and influence of the leader varies according to his ability to aid the group in achieving its goals.[7] Where the leader is appointed by a more

powerful group rather than being selected by his own group, the above generalizations must be qualified. For instance, if the goals of the subordinate group clash with those of the group by which he is appointed, he will be received not as leader, but as a representative of a different group.

3. *Normal Rules Guiding Group Behavior.* Along with the emerging set of power relations is the evolution of a normal set of "rules of the game," which specifies the conditions of interaction between group members. In other words, varying degrees of familiarity, influence, interaction and other relationships between members are sanctioned by the group according to an individual's role and position in the group hierarchy. Deviations from the rules and procedures by a member can lead to subtle but potent pressures by his fellow members to insure that the deviant "swings back into line."[7] Such pressures act quite differently on each person as a function of his status and personality, but they do act.

Identification with One's Group

The preceding three characteristics of group formation and operation—goals, leadership and norms—lead to varying degrees of identification with one's group. When feelings of identification are strong, the group is said to have high morale; it is highly cohesive.[8] The opposite is true when feelings of identification with group goals are low. Under circumstances of unacceptable power distribution or inappropriate norms, for example, the result is feelings of low morale, demoralization, low cohesion or possibly alienation. The greater the sense of identification a member has with his group, the greater are the pressures on him to follow, at times blindly, the direction and will of the group position.[9,10]

These are all common properties of organized groups. A representative of a group, whether leader or member, is compelled to acknowledge in some way these group properties as he comes in contact with members of other groups whose interests support or violate those of his own. For a representative to agree to actions which other members feel are contrary to group goals can result in his being seen to have acted in a betraying way, or in poor faith. On the other hand, acting effectively against opposition and in support of group purpose and goals, and consistent with internal norms and values, insures retention or enhancement of his status.[11]

The Relationship of the Organization Framework to Individual and Group Relations

The internal properties of a group are only one of the significant matters involved in understanding and managing intergroup relations. When the actions of individuals and groups are viewed within the framework of a complex organization, we can identify additional determinants of behavior.[12]

A Framework of Interdependent Organizational Subgroups

Consider the following circumstance in a large and complex organization: the total membership of the organization is subdivided into many smaller groups. Each subgroup has its own leadership and its own rules and regulations. Each has its own goals which may or may not be in accord with overall organizational goals.[13] Each operates with its own degree of cohesion which varies with feelings of failure or accomplishment.[14] In an organization, these groups are interdependent with one another. They may be interdependent in performing a complex task requiring coordination of effort, in geographical proximity, or in terms of the reward system of the organization. Differences among them immediately become apparent to members.

Comparison between groups. Perception of differences between groups leads spontaneously to a comparison and to a "we-they" orientation.[5] Attention quickly focuses on similarities and differences. Furthermore, these spontaneous comparisons are intensified by the tendency of higher levels of authority to evaluate and reward by group comparison. For example, group incentive plans, awarding of plaques or other symbols of organization success to the highest selling group, the group with the highest safety record, and so forth, all tend to high-light group differences.[15] Thus, in a sense, "winning" and "losing" groups are held up for all to see. The organization's rationale is that a spirit of competition is a "healthy" motivating force for achieving organizational ends.[16, 17]

On the other hand, these comparisons sometimes lead to the discovery of common values and mutually supportive opportunities which can result in greater intergroup cohesion. When this happens, it is possible to achieve an intergroup atmosphere that can lead to effective problem-solving and cooperation. Feelings of shared responsibility may then lead to identification with overall organizational goals, and to heightened recognition of similarities with resulting reduction of differences and tensions between them.[18]

Pitfalls of comparisons across groups. There is no assurance, however, that comparisons between groups inevitably lead to favorable outcomes. Instead, in the process of comparison, groups may discover discrepancies in treatment and privileges,[19] points of view, objectives, values, and so on. Then a different process unfolds. Comparisons tend to become invidious.[5] Differences are spotlighted and come to the focus of attention. Distortions in perception occur which favor the ingroup and deprecate the outgroup.[20, 21, 22] Each group finds in the other's performances an obstacle to attaining some or all of its own goals. When this situation extends beyond some critical point, each group may view the other as a threat to its own survival. At this point, disagreements are seen as permanent and inevitable, and the only possible resolution seems to lie in defeat of the other group in order to gain one's own objectives. Then all of the tools of common power struggles are brought into play.[23]

The manner in which representatives of groups interact, then, is colored by the background and history of agreements or disagreements of the groups they represent. The forces involved are powerful. The individual group's representative does not act only in terms of his job description or his specific background of training. Nor does he act solely within the context of his position within the group. Rather, he must be governed to some extent, depending on circumstances, by pre-existing relationships between the group he represents and the opposing group or representative of it that he is addressing.

Evaluated in terms of the forces acting in intergroup life, effective management of intergroup relations is a dimension of management that requires more analysis, more theory, and more skills than has been traditional in industrial life. To gain the necessary perspective, managers must focus not only on effective methods of resolving intergroup differences, but also on dysfunctional methods which lead to undesirable and disruptive side effects. Many dysfunctional methods for resolving conflicts have become common. These common practices have become embedded in the traditions of groups and organizations and must be understood to avoid their unthoughtful repetition.

THREE BASIC ASSUMPTIONS TOWARD INTERGROUP DISAGREEMENT

Three basic assumptions or attitudes toward intergroup disagreements and its management can be identified.

1. *Disagreement is Inevitable and Permanent*

One identifiable basic assumption is that disagreement is inevitable and permanent. When *A* and *B* disagree, the assumption is that the disagreement must be resolved in favor of *A* or in favor of *B*, one way or the other. Under this assumption there seems to be no other alternative. If two points of view are seen to be mutually exclusive, and if neither party is prepared to capitulate, then any of three major mechanisms of resolution may be used:

A. *Win-lose* power struggle to the point of capitulation by one group.

B. Resolution through a *third-party* decision.

C. Agreement *not* to determine the outcome, namely, *fate* arbitration.

2. *Conflict Can Be Avoided Since Interdependence Between Groups is Unnecessary*

A second orientation to intergroup relations rests on the assumption that while intergroup disagreement is not inevitable, neither is intergroup agreement possible. If these assumptions can be made, then interdependence is not necessary. Hence, when points of conflict arise between groups, they can be resolved by reducing the interdependence between parties. This reduction of interdependence may be achieved in three ways.

A. One group withdrawing from the scene of action.

B. Maintaining, or substituting *indifference* when it appears there is a conflict of interest.

C. *Isolating* the parties from each other; or the parties isolating themselves.

All of these (A, B, and C) share in common the maintenance of independence, rather than any attempt to achieve interdependence.

3. *Agreement and Maintaining Interdependence is Possible*

The third orientation to intergroup disagreement is that agreement is possible and that a means of resolving it must be found. Resolving conflict in this way is achieved by smoothing over the conflict while retaining interdependence. For example, visible though trivial reference may be made to overall organizational goals to which both parties are in some degree committed. Then attention is shifted away from real issues with surface harmony maintained. Alternatively, agreement may be achieved by bargaining, trading, or compromising. In a general sense, this is splitting the difference that separates the parties while at the same time retaining their interdependence. Finally, an effort may be made to resolve the disagreement by a genuine problem-solving approach. Here the effort is not devoted to determining who is right and who is wrong. Nor is it devoted to yielding something to gain something. Rather, a genuine effort is made to discover a creative resolution of fundamental points of difference.

As mentioned earlier, each of these three orientations is related to another dimension which determines the specific approach to be used in managing disagreement. This dimension might be pictured as extending from a *passive* attitude or low stakes to an *active* orientation involving high stakes.

FRAMEWORK FOR VIEWING INTERGROUP CONFLICT

Figure 1 pictures the possibilities within each of the three major orientations just described. These orientations (three vertical columns in Figure 1) are:

1. Conflict inevitable. Agreement impossible.

2. Conflict not inevitable, yet agreement not possible.

3. Agreement possible in spite of conflict.

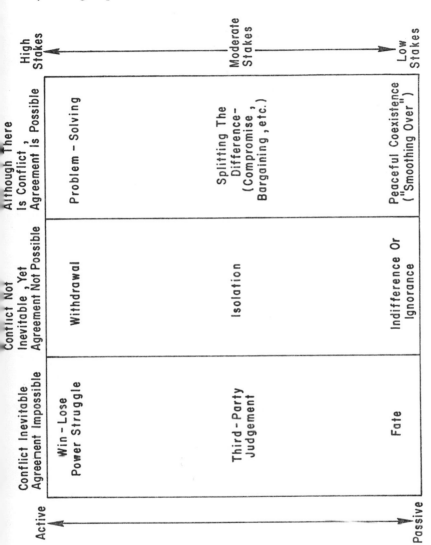

FIGURE 1. The three basic assumptions toward intergroup disagreements and their management.

At the bottom of each orientation is the method of resolution likely to be used where stakes in the outcome are low. The middle shows mechanisms employed where stakes in the outcome are moderate, and the upper end shows mechanisms likely to be adopted where stakes in the outcome of the conflict are high.

All the approaches in the left-hand orientation (column) *presume a condition of win-lose between the contesting parties.* Fate strategies come into force when stakes in the outcome are low, arbitration when the stakes are moderate, and win-lose power struggles when the stakes are high.

The right-hand vertical column of the graph reflects three opposite approaches to resolving disagreement. These approaches assume that though disagreement is present, agreement can be found. The most passive orientation here is identified as "smoothing over." This approach involves such well-known cultural phenomena as efforts to achieve intergroup cohesion and co-existence without really solving problems. The assumption is that somehow or another, peaceful co-existence will arise and that people will act in accordance with it.

The more active agreement contains the element of splitting differences. This is a more positive (active) approach than smoothing over differences, but it leaves much to be desired for it often produces only temporary resolution.

In the upper right-hand corner is the orientation of problem solving. This position identifies the circumstances under which the contesting parties search out the rationale of their agreements as well as the bases of their disagreements. It also identifies the causes for reservations and doubts of both parties. Here, the parties work toward the circumstances which will eliminate reservations. This climate affords the opportunity to actively explore means for achieving true agreement on issues without 'smoothing over' or compromising differences.

The middle column which utilizes such methods as withdrawal, isolation and indifference or ignorance is discussed in complete detail in Chapter 6.

SUMMARY

The behavior of organization members in relation to each other is, at the least, determined by one of three sets of forces:

1.   Job responsibilities.

2.   Social backgrounds represented in such considerations as training and experience.

3.   The set of complex forces acting on them by virtue of their active memberships in different groups.

This chapter has been concerned primarily with the third set of forces.

As a group member, whether leader or member, *an individual is a representative of his group* whenever he interacts with others in different groups, provided the groups are in some way interdependent. As a representative, a group member's opinions and attitudes are shaped by the goals, norms and values he shares with others of his group. Normal rules of conduct and the expectations of others in his group do not allow him to act independently of his group's interests when areas of disagreement arise between his group and another.

Large organizations are composed of many small groups. Because of the size, complexity and nature of present-day organizations, group comparisons, particularly of an invidious character, are bound to occur. Under such circumstances, differences, rather than similarities and commonness of purpose, are highlighted, with conflict the inevitable result. The result is that organizational needs for interdependence and cooperation among groups are not met as well as they might have been, had managerial personnel applied greater understanding to intergroup relations.

Three basic orientations to intergroup disagreement, in combination with these different degrees of 'stake in the outcome,' and their accompanying approaches for achieving resolution were outlined. In later chapters we will examine in depth these basic orientations and the effective and dysfunctional methods of achieving resolution between contesting parties.

References

1. Sheppard, H. L. "Approaches to conflict in American industrial Sociology." *Brit. J. Sociol.*, 5, 1954, 324-341.

2. Blake, R. R. "Psychology and the Crisis of Statesmanship." *Amer. Psychologist*, 14, 1959, 87-94. Blake, R. R. and Mouton, J. S., *Group Dynamics—Key to Decision Making.* Houston: Gulf Publishing Co., 1961, 87.

3. Faris, R. E. L. "Interaction Levels and Intergroup Relations." In. M. Sherif, (Ed.) *Intergroup Relations and Leadership.* New York: John Wiley and Sons, Inc., 1962, 24-45.

4. Stogdill, R. M. Intragroup-Intergroup Theory and Research. In M. Sherif (ed.), *Intergroup Relations and Leadership.* New York: John Wiley and Sons, Inc., 1962, 48-65.

5. Sherif, M. and Sherif C. *Outline of Social Psychology* (revised). New York: Harper & Bros., 1956.

6. Cartwright, D. and Zander, A. *Group Dynamics: Research and Theory,* (2nd edition). Evanston, Illinois: Row, Peterson & Co., 1960.

7. Hamblin, R. L., Miller, K. and Wiggins, J. A. "Group Morale and Competence of the Leader," *Sociometry,* 24, (3), 1961, 295-311.

8. Sherif, M. and Sherif, C. W. *Outline of Social Psychology* (revised), *op. cit.*

9. Cartwright, D. and Zander, A. *Group Dynamics: Research and Theory,* (1st edition). Evanston, Ill. Row, Peterson & Co., 1953.

10. Gerard, H. B. "The Anchorage of Opinion in Face to Face Groups," *Human. Relat.,* 7, 1954, 313-325; and Kelley, H. H. and Volkart, E. H., "The Resistance to Change of Group Anchored Attitudes," *Amer. Sociol. Rev.,* 17, 1952, 453-465.

11. Pryer, M. W., Flint, A. W., and Bass, B. M. "Group Effectiveness and Consistency of Leadership," *Sociometry,* 25, (4), 1962, 391; and Sherif, M. and Sherif, C. W. *Outline of Social Psychology* (revised), *op. cit.*

12. Arensberg, C. H. "Behavior and Organization: Industrial Studies." In J. H. Rohrer and M. Sherif (eds.), *Social Psychology at the Crossroads.* New York: Harper & Bros., 1951.

13. Cooper, H. C. "Perception of Subgroup Power and Intensity of Affiliation with a Large Organization." *Amer. Sociol Rev.,* 26, (2) 1961, 272-274.

14. Wolman, B. B. "Impact of Failure on Group Cohesiveness," *J. Soc. Psychol.,* 51, 1960, 409-418.

15. Sherif, M. and Sherif, C. W. *Outline of Social Psychology* (revised), *op. cit.*

16. Sayles, L. R. "The Impact of Incentives on Intergroup Relations: Management and Union Problem," *Personnel,* 28, 1952, 483-490.

17. Spriegel, W. R. and Lansburgh, R. H. *Industrial Management,* (5th edition). New York: John Wiley, 1955; and Strauss, G. and Sayles, L. R. *Personnel.* Englewood Cliffs, N. J.: Prentice-Hall, 1960.

18. Sherif, M. "Superordinate Goals in the Reduction of Intergroup Conflict," *Amer. J. Sociol.,* 43, 1958, 394-356.

19. Strauss, G. "Group Dynamics and Intergroup Relations." In W. F. White (ed.), *Money and Motivation.* New York: Harper & Bros., 1955, 90-96.

20. Sherif, M. and Sherif, C. W. *Outline of Social Psychology* (revised), *op. cit.*

21. Cohen, A. R. "Upward Communication in Experimentally Created Hierarchies," *Human Relat.,* 11, 1958, 41-53; Kelley, H. H. "Communication in Experimentally Created Hierarchies," *Human Relat.,* 4, 1951, 39-56; and Thibaut, J. "An Experimental Study of the Cohesiveness of Under-Privileged Groups," *Human Relat.,* 3, 1950, 251-278.

22. Blake, R. R. and Mouton, J. S. "Comprehension of Own and Outgroup Position Under Intergroup Competition," *J. Confl. Resolut.,* 5, (3), 1961, 304-310.

2

The Win-Lose Orientation
To Intergroup Disagreement

A win-lose orientation to conflict is characterized by one basic element: the contesting parties see their interests to be mutually exclusive. No compromise is possible. One must fail at the price of the other's success. Because of this point of view, hope is abandoned of being able to appeal to each other on the basis of reason. The attitude is that the issue can only be decided by a contest of power, *by a third party* who possesses powers greater than either of them, or by *fate*.

Striking examples of industrial win-lose union-management contests are found in the annals of American industry.[1,2,3,4] Study of these demonstrates American industry's substantial failure to understand the dynamics and consequences of intergroup win-lose power struggles. The actions and reactions of the protagonists in such disputes often deepen antagonism and destroy all avenues of resolution rather than contribute to intergroup problem-solving. Thus, it is apparent every manager should have an understanding of such intergroup win-lose power struggles in order to constructively deal with them.

A series of experiments dealing with intergroup disagreement were conducted to investigate win-lose orientations with most of these experiments being undertaken in industry. This chapter reviews and summarizes the experimental procedures, the results obtained, and the generalizations about intergroup behavior they produced.

EXPERIMENTAL APPROACHES TO STUDYING INTERGROUP CONFLICT

The prototype intergroup experiment was designed and executed by Sherif.[5] In his studies, two autonomous groups of children were brought into competition. The situation was that there was no realistic possibility of avoiding confrontation.[6] First ingroup and then intergroup, phenomena generated by the competitive circumstances were studied. Then after competition, effective and ineffective conditions for reducing competitive tensions and conflict between groups were identified and evaluated.

Succeeding experiments were also conducted with adults drawn from industrial organizations.[7] Each of the thirty experiments in the latter series extended over a two-week period. Each experiment dealt with a different win-lose aspect.

The experiments were carried out over several years and involved approximately 1,000 subjects. The subjects were members of more than 150 almost-identical groups which were matched according to personal characteristics and other relevant dimensions. Each study has been repeated, as necessary, to verify conclusions.

Experimental Setting

The setting for these industrial experiments can be described as follows: twenty to thirty executives came together for two weeks to discuss interpersonal and intergroup relations in their own behavior as well as those characteristic of their organization. Aspects of interpersonal and intergroup relations were first experienced by the executives in a series of controlled laboratory experiments. The experiments were then evaluated and analyzed as a basis for generalizations about organizational dynamics.

Ingroup Phase

During the first meetings as each group tackled the conference problems, some degree of ingroup cohesiveness developed, along with some frustration and fears that it was floundering. Concern lest the other group might be doing a better job was expressed in cautious questioning and kidding of members at coffee breaks and meal times. The natural trend of this intergroup comparison was in a negative and invidious direction.

Intergroup Phase

The competitive feelings underlying intergroup comparison created an eagerness in both groups to engage in a contest. Hence, the necessary conditions were present for studying the dynamics of intergroup conflict.

At this point, each group was provided an identical problem for which it was to find the "best" solution. The solutions were then evaluated with one being chosen as the better of the two. Because the atmosphere of the conferences induced deep involvement of the participants, this test of their groups' performance had psychological reality for them.

The realism and similarity between the setting of the win-lose experiments and situations of industrial conflict can be seen. Similar situations are often found when, with fixed positions, union and management approach bargaining, grievances handling, complaints or other situations; that is, where the intention of each side is *not to compromise, but to win.*

Typical examples of win-lose positions in present union-management relations can also be seen in those areas concerned with the contracting of work, work flexibility, maintenance of craft lines, and so on.

DYNAMICS OF INTERGROUP WIN-LOSE POWER STRUGGLES

Summarized now are generalizations from experiments for understanding win-lose intergroup disagreement. Also summarized are steps, derived from these generalizations, that can lead to more healthy intergroup problem-solving relations.

Introduction of Competition

At the point where intergroup competitiveness emerges in the experiments, the fundamental significance of the win-lose dynamic appears. When the goal, "to win," is accepted by a group, it has a spontaneous power to mobilize team effort and to give it character and direction.[8, 9, 10] The consequences for ingroup [11, 12, 13] and intergroup life are substantial when the goal of each side is to win. Some of these predictable consequences are discussed now.

Closing ranks and increasing cohesion. Under competitive circumstances as described, we can see a variety of highly predictable and measurable phenomena. One is lift in cohesion. The rule is, when an adversary approaches, members close ranks, either to defend or to attack. Spirits go up! Former disagreements within the group tend to be put aside. Members pitch in. They pull together for the common goal of victory.[14, 15]

Exciting as it seems to march together toward victory, the urge to win appears to be primitive and basic. Here is a first condition of group tension. Dispute among members which is often the raw material of creative thinking,[16] and can lead to the reexamination and enrichment of an initial group position, tends to be snuffed out. The failure of any group member to go along with the group position will arouse group pressures toward conformity after the group reaches a certain point of entrenchment. In extreme cases of group unison, deviation may lead to excommunication and even expulsion of those who resist.[17]

Leadership consolidation. The presence of a "pecking order" among group members is well known. For reasons of superior logic, or expression, or because of stronger motivation to win, some voices carry more weight than others in defining group direction and character. Prior to competition when there is neither time nor output pressure, power relations are loose and rather poorly developed. Few members feel much responsibility for their group's performance.

But what happens among team members when clear and sharp competitive forces are exerted? The stakes get higher. As a result, one's personal pride and reputation merge with the group's reputation. Some members begin to exercise more weight than they had previously[18] and individual members become more distinguished. It may be that those who are able to talk better than others "come to the top." Often, it is those for whom the thought of victory in a fight carries particular relish. In the extreme, the result can be a complete takeover by one or a few persons.[19] The others, who may be less able or aggressive, or more dependent, tend to fall into line—sometimes with apparent satisfaction at "throwing in their support." To avoid the responsibility for possible defeat or to hide disagreement, still others "bite their tongues" and take little or no active part.[20]

What then, are the consequences? There definitely is group unity and accomplishment. A clear power structure is established, and quickly. But, if those who control the major lines of group effort fail to exercise their influence in ways that recognize the "legitimate" rights of others, the seeds for internal strife are sown and will germinate when the intergroup competition is over. As we will see, defeat becomes the fertile soil that nourishes the growth and development of splintering and discord. By and large, people do not know how to cope with such strains in group life. Serious barriers to future ingroup cooperation may have been created unwittingly by the impelling urge to win under conditions of an intergroup win-lose conflict.

Positions Contrasted: Own Position Enhanced; Adversary's Downgraded

Each group's decision and position is referred to as its product.

After the product created by the groups has taken shape and has been compared with that of a contending group, members quickly reassay their attitudes toward their own solution and toward that of the other group as well. But judgments concerning the quality of competing products are colored by membership considerations.[21] Thus, the direction of distortion is clear—it is for one's own group's product to be judged superior to the other's. This is true even in the face of facts that measurable quality differences do exist between them. Group members, in other words, strongly identify with their own product. They rationalize shortcomings in their own product and downgrade the competitor's product.[21]

In intergroup relations, win-lose conflict distorts realistic judgment.[22] Heightened disagreement tends to obliterate objectivity. Yet, as will be seen later, objectivity is a primary condition of intergroup problem-solving. When win-lose attitudes reach such a degree that the parties are unable to make realistic appraisals, then the possibilities of future cooperation have been reduced or eliminated.

Attack and Counterattack: Paper Bombs as Substitutes for Bullets

After studying the two positions, groups interact through representatives who will determine a winner and a loser. But before their final decision, a phase of public debate between representatives is provided for clarifying similarities and differences between the two positions. During this stage, questions put to each group are answered through their representatives.

The motivation underlying the questions representatives ask each other is revealed by the content of the questions which group members write and hand to their representatives. Are they intended to clarify? For the most part, they are not. They are couched so as to belittle the competitor's position, to cast doubt on its validity, and to demonstrate its inferiority to one's own group's position.[15]

Rather than reducing the conflict and increasing objectivity, intergroup contact for purposes of clarification under the conditions just described, tends to have the opposite effect. Conflict is intensified. Subjectivity is promoted. Suspicion of the "motivation of others" is increased.[23]

Negative Stereotypes Concerning One's Adversary

When contacts between two groups are competitive and mutually frustrating, the interactions of groups through their representatives lead to strong stereotype formations. Members of each group develop negative attitudes. They express hostility toward members of the other group.[24]

These hostile expressions, in turn, have an accelerating and provocative effect. The stereotypes are saturated with negative emotions. The consequence of provocation tends to be counter-provocation. This, in turn, leads to the further intensification of conflict. The end result is erosion of mutual respect and confidence in the constructiveness of the other's intentions.

The Perception of Representative Personality

Group members tend to select as their representative, an individual who is seen as "strong." His strength lies in dominating the group, resisting conformity pressures, and facing up to problems rather than running away from them.[25]

As persons, representatives are usually viewed quite objectively by the members of both groups—*before* they begin to interact. They are seen as reasonably mature, intelligent, independent, well-intended human beings. As interaction proceeds, however, the process of provocation and reaction soon destroys the initial perceptions. One's own representative is seen as manfully defending his group against hostile attack. The representative of the other group shows himself to be less and less mature, less well-intentioned, less intelligent, etc., Group members are blind to the fact that representative behavior is largely determined by the forces of group membership and win-lose conflict. They see the opposing representative's behavior as governed by more or less despicable personality traits; their own representative's behavior as governed by praiseworthy personality traits.

Intellectual Distortions

As mentioned, group members tend to develop negative feelings and emotions toward their adversary. But, is this the sole source of the problem, or is there something beyond? Does competition affect one's capacity to think, to understand, and to comprehend? The answer is "yes," and the effect on mental functions is insidious.[26, 27] How is this demonstrated?

Each group is allowed to study the other's product until all members indicate, with essentially complete subjective certainty, that they have achieved intellectual understanding of their adversary's position. Then, an objective test covering the positions of the contending groups is introduced. The analysis of test results is enlightening. It shows how win-lose attitudes can contaminate objective thinking and it points out something of the character of the resulting distortions.

Commonalities minimized, differences highlighted. On the test just described, similarities in group products are virtually ignored, but areas of difference are highlighted. The most common error found is to misidentify items in both products as having been in only one. In other words, many items are seen as uniquely one's own product, even when they are present in both products. *While group members correctly recognize that such items belong to their own group's position, they fail to see that the same items are contained in the adversary's position.* As a result commonalities tend to be overlooked and disparities increased when groups are in competition. Consequently, needless barriers to understanding and agreement are created.[28]

Comprehension of own proposal greater than understanding of competitor's proposal. In comparison with common items, the distinctive ones—that is, items contained only in the position of the other group, but not in both—are generally recognized correctly more frequently than any other type. But even then distortions are present. Group members identify elements distinctive to their own position with greater accuracy than they do items which are distinctive *only* in the adversary's position.[15]

Without exploring in greater detail the motivation for these distortions, it can be said that cognitive "blind spots" are not entirely due to familiarity with one's own position. To be sure, difference in familiarity with the two products is a factor. Beyond familiarity, however, differences in the degree of understanding are due only to group membership, feelings of personal ownership, group identification, and defensiveness under the threat of defeat.[15]

Resolution of Difference Through the Use of Representatives

What is the character of group deliberations when representatives meet to determine a winner and loser?

Loyalty of representatives. A representative who exercises impartiality and takes an objective point of view is in danger of losing for his group since he might have to admit that a competitor's position is superior to his own. Thus, loyalty pressures often overwhelm logic. Subjectively, most representatives feel that they are acting out of intellectual convictions and logic, and that loyalty to one's own point of view is not a factor. But, even though a representative feels he is being objective in his own judgment, he rarely is.

Despite intellectual convictions, representatives soon fall to parrying, jabbing, and feinting and probing for weaknesses in the other's position rather than pursuing the interaction objectively and logically. The urge to win becomes immediately paramount and intellectual objectivity disappears.

In these experiments, deadlock is the most frequent result from representative negotiation.[29] As Stephen Decatur, in 1816 said, "Our country! In her intercourse with foreign nations, may she always be in the right; but our country, right or wrong!"

The motive "to win" produces behavior which is incomprehensible when viewed from the standpoint of the psychophysics of comparative judgments only. If problem-solving is to lead to effective and mutually satisfactory solutions, groups seeking to resolve conflicts must substitute objectivity for considerations based on loyalty and "win."[30]

Hero-traitor dynamics. Underlying the representative's sense of intellectual conviction, then, are the emotional pressures of loyalty—his personal satisfaction with his own group's product, and his derogation of the other. And underlying his identification with one group at the expense of the other is the *hero-traitor dynamic*.

A traitor is a group member in good standing who, on contacting the adversary, capitulates to the enemy's position. He loses for his group. A hero, on the other hand, is a person who wins for his group by vanquishing his adversary. Being tagged a traitor means loss of face or prestige,[31] being ridiculed and, in the extreme, being expelled from one's group. On the other hand, being a hero brings rewards of applause, warmth, increased status and heightened prestige. Yet, the behavior required to be heroic can vary from the actions requiring objectivity and problem-solving. Equally unfortunate, behavior based on objective problem-solving may be withheld deliberately to avoid the *traitor* trap. Deadlock, though it does not carry with it the elevation in status accorded a hero, at least is one way to avoid the traitor trap.

The Method of Determining Victory and Defeat

Experiments as described, permit study of additional intergroup problems, including resolution through third party arrangements. Since it is difficult to determine a winner through representatives, an impartial judge is used to produce a verdict.

The judge examines and evaluates each group's product against preestablished criteria of excellence. Based on his evaluation, one group is judged to be the winner; the other the loser. He explains his criteria of judgment for evaluating both products and presents his decision.

Impact of Victory and Defeat on Group Leadership: Consolidation vs. Replacement

In winning groups, those who led the fight to victory are congratulated. Their positions in the "pecking order" are strengthened and enhanced. Those who follow them to victory tend to become even more dependent on the leaders for future direction and guidance.

In defeated groups, ingroup fighting and splintering occurs, which results in cliques and factions as members track down the culprits who led them astray.[5] The seeds of discontent that were planted when certain members "took over" and doubts of less vocal ones now spring to life. A common result is a pecking order shift, with those who, prior to defeat, enjoyed highest status losing it, and those who were granted least status moving up in the pecking order. Former leaders are replaced, on occasion, because their ability and integrity are in question. Feeling unfairly attacked by their own group, the replaced leaders often fight back to justify their actions and to remain influential.

Group mentality. Group mentality is dramatically different in winning and losing groups. This is apparent not only in reactions to the judge and to the representatives, but also in the atmosphere of the groups themselves.[15]

Members of victorious groups feel the glow of victory. The dominant theme is complacency stemming from success. There is a "fat and happy" atmosphere as members coast and rest on their laurels. It does not occur to the winning group to critique their efforts and to look for better ways of working. They tend to let down and enjoy the fruits of their success.

On the other hand, the defeated group tends to become "lean and hungry." The atmosphere fills with tension that must be discharged. Members describe their interactions as "digging" activities, focused on ferreting out fallacies of operation that led to failure, and assigning responsibility for them.

A dramatic example of a defeated group was discussed in the following way by the *Wall Street Journal,* shortly after November 4, 1960. "The Republican Party, scarcely stopping to lick its wounds after a narrow national defeat, today enters a period of protracted, intense and possible disruptive civil war."[32]

Victory can promote complacency which fails to come to grips with future problems. Such complacency is no less disturbing, and perhaps even more detrimental, to intergroup health than is the destructive ingroup fighting often associated with defeat.[33]

Loss of capacity for empathy. Not only do victorious and defeated groups react differently to win-lose experience, but also the reactions of each are incomprehensible to the other. The complacency and self-congratulatory behavior of the winning group is seen as vainglorious by the members of the defeated group. Similarly, the sullen, defensive attitude of the defeated group is shocking to the members of the victorious group. Each asks, "How can those *others* take this trivial matter so seriously?"

The Win-Lose Trap

Immediately following the experiments in intergroup competition, the groups are sometimes asked to move almost immediately into situations requiring intergroup cooperation in the solution of a second problem. Almost invariably, they shortly find themselves working as antagonists rather than as collaborators. Feelings of competitiveness and mutually disparaging attitudes have become so deeply ingrained that members of one group cannot perceive the offerings of the other group as well-intended.

Only when the groups review the entire competition episode in detail, and together examine subjective attitudes of antagonism and how they were produced, as well as the objective data collected in the course of the experiment, are they able to regain perspective of themselves, their reactions, and the interrelationship. By analyzing and gaining insight into the background of their past behavior, it is possible for them to start working collaboratively across group lines.

Summary

The sequence of phenomena discussed is from intergroup competition experiments with the prevailing win-lose assumption that disagreement is inevitable. The experiments were conducted under artificially constructed conditions, although the experimental situations were psychologically real for the participants. The controlled laboratory situations highlighted and permitted measurement of a number of psychological and social aspects of win-lose conflict under circumstances where "disagreement is inevitable." The sequence of events, the dynamic aspects of intergroup conflict, the results and subsequent generalizations from these experiments will serve as a framework and foundation for the remainder of this book.

In succeeding chapters, which focus on intergroup relations in organizations, we will discuss and evaluate parallels between the experimental and actual intergroup win-lose conflicts.

References

1. Petro, S. *The Kohler Strike: Union Violence and Administrative Law*. Chicago: Henry Regnery Co., 1961; Selekman, B. "Varieties of Labor Relations." In Joseph Shister (ed.), *Readings in Labor Economics and Industrial Relations*. New York: Lippincott, 1951; Derber, M., Chalmers, W. E., Stagner, R. and Edelman, M. *The Local Union-Management Relationships*. Urbana, Ill.: Institute of Labor and Industrial Relations, University of Illinois, 1960; and Ross, A. M. and Hartman, P. T. *Changing Patterns of Industrial Conflict*. Institute of Industrial Relations, University of California, New York: John Wiley, 1960.

2. Sherif, M., Harvey, O. J., White, B. J., Hood, W. R. and Sherif, C. W. *Intergroup Conflict and Cooperation: The Robbers Cave Experiment*. Norman, Oklahoma: Institute of Group Relations, University of Oklahoma Book Exchange, 1961.

3. Sherif, M. and Sherif, C. W. *Groups in Harmony and Tension*. New York: Harper & Bros., 1953.

4. Blake, R. R. and Mouton, J. S. "The Intergroup Dynamics of Win-Lose Conflict and Problem-Solving Collaboration in Union-Management Relations." In M. Sherif (ed.), *Intergroup Relations and Leadership*. New York: John Wiley, 1962, 94-140.

5. Dashiell, J. F. "An Experimental Analysis of Some Group Effects," *J. Abnorm. Soc. Psychol.*, 25, 1930, 190-199; Hurlock, E. B. "The Use of Group Rivalry as an Incentive," *J. Abnorm. Soc. Psychol.*, 22, 1927, 278-290; and Maller, J. B. "Cooperation and Competition: An Experimental Study in Motivation," *Contrib. Educa.*, 384, New York: Columbia University, 1929.

6. Deutsch, M. "The Effects of Cooperation and Competition Upon Group Process: An Experimental Study," *Amer. Psychologist*, 4, 1949, 263-264; Grossack, M. M. "Some Effects of Cooperation and Competition Upon Small Group Behavior," *J. Abnorm. Soc. Psychol.*, 49, 1954, 341-348; and Hammond, L. K. and Goldman, M. "Competition and Non-competition and its Relationship to Individual and Group Productivity," *Sociometry*, 24, (1), 1961, 46-60.

7. Blake, R. R. and Mouton, J. S. *Group Dynamics—Key to Decision Making*. Houston: Gulf Publishing Co., 1961.

8. Sherif, M. and Sherif, C. W. *Outline of Social Psychology* (revised). New York: Harper & Bros., 1956; and Blake, R. R. and Mouton, J. S. "Comprehension of Own and Outgroup Positions Under Intergroup Competition," *J. Confl., Resolut.* 5, (3), 1961, 304-310.

9. Hewlett, Allen. "Nobody Cares How Tough You Have It," *Advanc. Mgmt.*, 21, (9), 1956, 27.

10. Schachter, S. "Deviation, Rejection and Communication," *J. Abnorm. Soc. Psychol.*, 46, 1951, 190-207.

11. Hamblin, R. L. "Leadership and Crisis," *Sociometry*, 21, 1958, 322-335.

12. Sherif, M. "Intergroup Relations and Leadership: Introductory Statement," In M. Sherif (ed.), *Intergroup Relations and Leadership, op. cit.*, 3-21.

13. Blake, R. R. and Mouton, J. S. "The Story Behind Intergroup Conflict." In *Group Dynamics—Key to Decision Making, op. cit.*

14. Blake, R. R. and Mouton, J. S. "Overevaluation of Own Group's Product in Intergroup Competition," *J. Abnorm. Soc. Psychol.*, 64, (3), 1962, 237-238.

15. Harvey, O. J. "An Experimental Investigation of Negative and Position Relationships Between Small Informal Groups Through Judgmental Indices." *Doctorate Dissertation,* University of Oklahoma, 1954.

16. Blake, R. R. and Mouton, J. S. "Comprehension of Own and Outgroup Positions Under Intergroup Competition," *op. cit.*

17. Deutsch, M. "The Effect of Motivational Orientation Upon Trust and Suspicion," *Human Relat.*, 13, 1960, 123-140.

18. Smythe, H. and Seidman, M. "Name Calling: A Significant Factor in Human Relations," *Human Relat.*, 6, 1957, 71-77.

19. Blake, R. R. and Mouton, J. S. "Perceived Characteristics of Elected Representatives," *J. Abnorm. Soc. Psychol.*, 62, (3), 1961, 693-695.

20. Cooper, E. and Jahoda, M. "The Evasion of Propaganda: How Prejudiced People Respond to Anti-prejudice Propaganda," *J. Psychol.*, 23, 1947, 15-25; and Kunarngo, R. and Das, J. P. "Differential Learning and Forgetting as a Function of the Social Frame of Reference," *J. Abnorm. Soc. Psychol.*, 61, 1960, 82-86.

21. Blake, R. R. and Mouton, J. S. "Comprehension of Points of Communality in Competing Solutions," *Sociometry*, 25, (1), 1962, 56-63.

22. Blake, R. R. and Mouton, J. S. "Comprehension of Own and Outgroup Positions Under Intergroup Competition," *op. cit.*; and Blake, R. R. and Mouton, J. S. "Comprehension of Points of Communality in Competing Solutions," *op. cit.*

23. *Ibid.*

24. Blake, R. R. and Mouton, J. S. "Loyalty of Representatives to Ingroup Positions During Intergroup Competition," *Sociometry*, 24, (2), 1961, 171-183.

25. Blake, R. R. "Psychology and the Crisis of Statesmanship," *Amer. Psychologist*, 14, 1959, 78-94.

26. Goffman, E. "On Face-work," *Psychiatry*, 18, 1955, 213-231.

27. Sherif, M., Harvey, O. J., White, B. J., Hood, W. R. and Sherif, C. W. *Intergroup Conflict and Cooperation: The Robbers Cave Experiment, op. cit.*

28. Blake, R. R. and Mouton, J. S. *Group Dynamics—Key to Decision Making, op. cit.*

29. *Wall Street Journal*, "GOP vs. GOP," 26, (93), Nov. 10, 1960, 1.

30. Blake, R. R. and Mouton, J. S. "Why Problem-Solving Between Groups Sometimes Fails," *Group Dynamics—Key to Decision Making.*

3

Win-Lose Power Struggles
In Industrial Life

In industry, one of the most common areas where examples of win-lose power struggles are found is in union-management relations.[1] These are not the only groups in industry which engage in win-lose power struggles, but because unions are semi-autonomous, legally constituted bodies, struggles between them and management can be made more public. Union-management situations where relations are more likely to be of equal power can more easily result in win-lose struggles than ones solely within management where a reservoir of power can be utilized by the group higher in the hierarchy. These latter struggles between groups that have no legitimate life outside the corporate structure, however, tend to stay hidden from the public eye. Our examples in this chapter are not only from the field of union-management relations but also from the less public fields of interdepartmental, headquarters-field and interplant conflict.

UNION AND MANAGEMENT RELATIONS

By no means are all union-management relations to be categorized as win-lose power struggles. In fact, today's unions and managements become engaged in such struggles only when normal relationships break down. Government legislation as well as those parties involved, expect union-management negotiations to be conducted under the condition where, "though disagreements are present, agreement is possible."

Normally there is an underlying conviction that a road to an agreement can somehow be found. Coupled with this assumption is the belief that the normal *procedures* for achieving agreement are in the right-hand area of the scale of Figure 1 rather than in the left-hand scale. That is, agreement is seen to be possible through the mechanisms of peaceful co-existence, bargaining, compromise, mediation or problem-solving.

However, bargaining problems do arise,[2] and it is possible, and indeed likely, for the parties eventually to lose faith in the possibility of finding agreement. There is a basic reason why bargaining in union-management negotiations so often deteriorates into a win-lose power struggle. Beneath the surface are widespread and deeply ingrained attitudes of mutual suspicion, antagonism and lack of empathy[3] on the parts of many managements and many unions. One such attitude, for example, is that there is an irresolvable and ideological conflict between the two. That is to say, many managements feel that unions are fundamentally antithetic to management goals. Correspondingly, unions harbor the belief that managements are basically antagonistic toward the existence of union organizations. Thus, the requirement that managements and unions "bargain in good faith" is often an external rather than internal requirement of interaction. The shared conviction of finding a road to agreement is rarer than one would expect, especially after reading the legislative requirements regarding union-management relationships.

Union-Management Win-Lose Power Struggles

The aim in this chapter is to examine the events that take

place in industry when the parties to a disagreement take a win-lose approach. Consider the following steps that are typical of union-management win-lose negotiations involving a struggle, where power is more or less equal.[4]

Drawing battle lines. In the intergroup conflict experiments, the characteristics of groups as they prepare for competition are comparable to those in union and management negotiating groups as they prepare for a battle.

Each side prepares a list of demands which are fixed rather than initial positions or orientations. Each attempts to foresee the tactics the other side will employ. Both groups develop strategies for cancelling out, undermining or rejecting the demands of the other. As though to increase rigidity of fixed positions, management demands are tested against the viewpoint of the top management group, not only to evaluate them from a business point of view, but also to assure each member of the bargaining committee that they will not be reversed. Then, all can develop convictions of the bargaining committee's position and its righteousness.

A similar kind of reinforcing action takes place within the union's central group. Positions are checked with relevant authorities outside of the union bargaining group for consistency with union objectives and to measure the likely support if things get to an impasse. The confirming of a position which can intensify antagonism[5] insures total backing from the larger groups represented by the negotiating subgroups.

Battle preparations. If both sides have formulated win-lose attitudes, then both are likely to spend a good deal of time in preparation for battle. That is, they look beyond the period of negotiations to the point where negotiations may break down and a strike is assured, in order to brace against it.

The planning done by each side tends to be based on the

belief that the other will capitulate. Often each believes the other will not go all the way to a strike when a showdown comes. Thus, with both sides holding convictions as to the rightness of it's positions, and with the added reinforcement that the opposition will back off rather than strike, the situation is set. If disagreement is seen as inevitable, the only realistic solution is to expect unconditional surrender, and total capitulation from the other.

Closing ranks. As in the experiments, union and management group members respond to the challenge hurled by the other. The contest is on. Once this condition is reached there is no point of return. Cohesion is likely to take a dramatic rise. Now a clear course of action is set. From this point forward, it becomes dangerous for individuals in either group to raise doubts. To express reservations as to the course of action being taken is to place one's membership in jeopardy. At this point the groups have closed ranks.

Fanning the Fires of Labor-Management Tension

As the union and management groups enter actual negotiations, they do so under the same conditions as representatives in the intergroup experiments.[6] That is to say, *their positions are fixed.* Their objectives are unchangeable. When a member of one side provokes one on the other side to an emotional reaction, he receives plaudits from his own members. The win-lose intent of each side readily communicates itself to the other side, reinforcing mutual suspicions.[7] Agreement becomes progressively less possible.

Underestimating and downgrading the enemy. At this point in negotiations, if the union leadership returns to reaffirm its position and to test the strength of its convictions, management searches for evidence of weaknesses. For example, the kind of evidence sought, although not accurate, may be low participation of the union membership at the hall.[8] Whenever there is a low turnout of union membership, management's interpretation is that the union is "weak"; that it lacks support. Often, management's strategy then is to press forward, even more strongly. In the event of a strike, management's assumption is that the union would be unable to control its membership and carry unresolved disagreements forward to an ultimate confrontation.

Reentrenchment. Referring again to the intergroup competition studies, we note a similar tactic employed by the representatives. The aim here is the same—to search out weaknesses of the other side and to exploit them. Also during this stage there are public announcements by each side. Often such announcements are intended to explain to the other group why it should capitulate and why its situation is "hopeless." In addition, there is usually a redeclaration of why each group will remain firm and consistent with its original positions. Management and union troops dig in for a long siege.

Highlighting Differences; Overlooking Commonalities

As would be anticipated from the intergroup competition experiments, union and management perceptions under win-lose conditions *focus more on differences in positions, less on similarities.*[9] Little or no attention is given to areas of commonality or areas of agreement. A typical example of this is the following:

A union had submitted to management the document from which it wished to bargain. Management took the union document and had it summarized in written form by the personnel department. The summary was then distributed to the management bargaining committee for study and analysis.

The point that needs emphasis here is the way in which management analyzed the union's proposals. Management's actions bore close resemblance to the mental operations characteristic of behavior under experimental conditions of win-lose intergroup competitiveness. Their assumptions were that, of necessity, the two group's positions were widely disparate; that disagreement was inevitable and that agreement was possible only through force.

No analysis whatsoever was given in the summary by the personnel department to those items in the union proposal which were identical with present union-company arrangements. Nor was attention paid to union points so similar to management's own position that they constituted only minor variations. By emphasizing differences, management failed to recognize, or at least it failed to remember and to place in true perspective, the similarities between its own positions and those of the union. Thus, a gross exaggeration of the magnitude of the separation between the two groups was created.

The management bargaining committee studied in detail the summary document. At no time, however, did the bargaining committee or any individual member study the original union proposal. Through the disregard of similarities and overemphasis on differences developed by the personnel department, the degree of actual agreement was grossly underestimated while the amount of perceived difference was increased out of proportion. In this way management could be fully reinforced in its convictions that union demands compelled inevitable disagreement.

Emphasis on Union and Management Personalities

As noted in the description of the representatives' perceptions in the intergroup competition experiments, the character structure or personalities of members on each side of the bargaining table are brought into question.[10] Win-lose conditions produce in management's description of union officers such adjectives as "stupid," "ill-willed," "disloyal," "unintelligent," "lacking in judgment," "unwilling (or unable) to weigh the pros and cons of a position," and "hopeless." The union, in turn, used such terms as "overbearing," "cold," "thoughtless," "manipulative," "calculating," and "deceitful" to depict management personnel. Personality explanation is a fallacy discovered in experimental intergroup competition. However, personality explanation *is not perceived as a fallacy but as reality* in actual win-lose struggles between union and management. The fallacy is seeing a person according to "what he is" and not recognizing the extent his behavior is consistent with membership requirements placed on him because of the win-lose nature of the intergroup relationship.

The preceding example demonstrates the manner in which win-lose power struggles in intergroup relationships insure that disagreements *will be inevitable*. The final result of the sequence just described, where the positions are "dug in," frequently is a strike. At this point the weapons used in the battle are most likely to be economic (situations of extreme bitterness may involve resort to force) to break the deadlock.

Additional phenomena arise during a strike and provide even wider avenues of study.[11] Generally, however, these are only extensions, often exaggerated, of what already has been described. They include inflaming public opinion, pointing out the malicious intent of the adversary, and a number of other win-lose phenomena.

What is relevant here, however, are the consequences that are likely to arise once a strike is resolved under conditions of victory and defeat. Let us look at them briefly.

Emergence of the Victor-Vanquished Phenomena

Fate of the vanquished. As would be predicted, union officers have difficulty surviving and achieving reelection once defeat results from a strike being broken. Similarly, replacement or transfer of responsible management officials by higher authority is likely to follow a severe defeat to management in its union negotiations.

Consolidation in the victor's camp. On the other side of the picture is the victor. Take an example where a union has called a strike and has been able to sustain its strength and extract capitulation from management. A result is that union leadership consolidates its position of strength with its own membership. By sticking to its guns, the union leadership is able to win its demands. Under these circumstances, union leadership is seen to have had the wisest judgment and is acclaimed by union members for having given good direction. It is seen as possessing the caliber and character of leadership needed for the road ahead.

The same thing can be seen in a victorious management group if the labor relations manager has successfully countered the tactics of an effective strike. That is, if he designed the strategy that eventually forced the union to capitulate. In this situation, the actions of the labor relations manager are likely to be judged as sound and wise by those he serves. His tactical maneuverings are seen to contain the key for achieving increased strength in the future.

Consistent with experimental findings, then, it is frequently possible to see two basic phenomena in the post victory-defeat reactions. One is *leadership replacement among the vanquished*; the other is *leadership consolidation among the victors*.

INTERGROUP CONFLICT WITHIN THE MANAGEMENT ORGANIZATION.

As mentioned, union-management relations are not the only examples of intergroup conflict in industry. There are numerous situations of win-lose intergroup fights and disagreements between line and staff components[12] or at high levels of organizations. Disputes are found between sales and manufacturing or other departments,[13] between autonomous divisions or diversified companies, or various other cleavages in organizations.[14]

These are so common as to be well within the experience of most readers. To place them in context, however, we will offer a few brief descriptions.

In-Plant Win-Lose Struggles

Perhaps most relevant at this point is an examination of the routine everyday intergroup win-lose problems of organizational life.[15]

As an example, a manufacturing division of a large company, through the agency of a special study, discovered severe problems in instrument development and maintenance. The problem of updating instrumentation seemed so important to some members of top management that a new instrument department under a new division was proposed. Both the engineering department head and the maintenance department head were opposed to this proposition. Reorganization meant that each department would need to release a certain segment of its organization to create a third. Acting as a coalition, the two department heads proposed to higher management, and won, an arrangement whereby an instrument development section would be created in the engineering department and an instrument maintenance section would be created in the maintenance department.

Up to this point in the example, the two departments appeared to be cooperating. At least, they agreed to a compromise solution to the conflict-of-interest problem between them. However, compromise was possible only because both groups would have suffered defeat had the proposal for a third department been accepted.

Immediately after adopting the compromise solution, the engineering department head instructed the newly created supervisor of the instrument development section how to conduct himself in his relations with the instrument maintenance group in the other department. In effect he said, "This arrangement is hopeless—the entire instrument development and maintenance responsibility should rest in the engineering department. We must do everything possible to demonstrate that it can't work this way so that we don't waste a whole year getting the entire operation into this department." Resultant sabotage, recriminations and politics ended in the eventual transfer of the instrument maintenance section to the engineering department. As expected, there followed a sense of complete defeat to the maintenance department. But as far as engineering was concerned, a substantial new colony in a much larger empire was on its way to being built.

The aftermath of this win-lose struggle was a severe deterioration in the relations between the engineering and maintenance departments, with the result that operations in both departments suffered.

FUNDAMENTAL ATTRIBUTES OF WIN-LOSE CONFLICT

Though most examples of in-company strife are different in texture and context, they bear certain fundamental attributes in common. These attributes need to be identified and examined more closely as they are general characteristics of win-lose situations.

Disagreement is Seen to be Inevitable

Win-lose dispute is based on the assumption that disagreement is inevitable. All of the common attributes found in experimental situations and in intergroup conflict in organizations flow automatically from the basic assumption that disagreement is inevitable. Hence, the first question that we must ask is, "What conditions arise from the conviction that disagreement is inevitable?" Belief in the inevitability of win-lose conflict seems to rest on any one of three conditions: (1) personalities, (2) ideological differences, and (3) the economics of scarcity. Let us discuss briefly each of these in more detail.

1. *Personalities.* The first condition of inevitable disagreement is that the personalities on the other side of the conflict are seen to be evil.[16] Their actions are said to be motivated by malicious intent. Once this proposition is granted, the inevitability of disagreement is clear since it is believed that personalities are unchangeable and independent of group affiliation. In the union-management context, this assumption often leads to management's efforts to find a way to replace "bad" union leaders with new ones who might be better.

However, as demonstrated by the intergroup-competition experiments, the apparent personality of the representative is more validly a product of the win-lose conflict of the parties. The behavior of the spokesman is, to a significant degree, a reaction to the win-lose behavior by the other aggressive party. Such hostile reactions reinforce the counter-beliefs that the personalities of the parties are unchangeable and evil. In this way, the inevitability of disagreement is reaffirmed.

2. *Ideological differences.* The second belief is that the parties are separated by unresolvable, ideological differences.[17]

Consider the example of the conflict surrounding the instrumentation section in the engineering department. The point of view of the engineering department was that proper instrumentation was *only* possible when sound engineering and scientific acumen and training were applied to the problem. The fact that this belief was held firmly by the engineering department precluded examination of alternative possibilities. The only choice open was to place the maintenance people under the direct control of the engineering people. Hence, taking the win-lose approach for the "good" of the organization seemed a "natural" result.

3. *The economics of scarcity.* A third condition of inevitable disagreement is lodged in scarcity. The assumption here is that there is not enough to go around and that, "We must fight to obtain our share." Thus, humanity is sub-divided into two groups—the "haves" and "have-nots," who are engaged in inevitable conflict.

In America the emphasis on material scarcity has been somewhat reduced by improved technology. However, a kind of economics of psychological scarcity has taken its place. Prestige, acceptance, influence, recognition and a kind of freedom of self-determination are the rewards that are now in scarce supply.

Effects of Either-Or Orientations

The three preceding alternative conditions of win-lose struggles have a single common feature. They polarize the world into two-value orientations. There are the good guys and the bad guys; the good values and the evil values; the "haves" and the "have-nots." The important question seems to be, "Which side are you on?"

Polarization of thinking is a hallmark of win-lose conflict. It oversimplifies problems and dehumanizes the participants in dispute, as in the hostile debates between representatives. Truth is of no concern. The object is to win. At the same time that the over-simplification of win-lose conflict leads to narrow and stereotypical thinking during disagreement, it also increases cohesion within each of the conflicting groups. By giving each of them a simple rallying cause, the combination of black-white thinking and self-righteousness leads to a deep conviction about the inevitability and permanence of disagreement. Thus, all other alternatives are eliminated, save the alternative of fighting it out.

Reinforcement of Beliefs Through the Mechanism of the Self-Fulfilling Prophecy

For these and other reasons, it is clear that the belief in the inevitable disagreement is also reinforced by evidences of validation in what is really a "self-fulfilling prophecy." Once it is taken for granted that the outgroup is alien and ill-intentioned, actions to meet and to cope with such behavior only evoke more of it. History is replete with examples of how a "justified" action by one side provoked a counteraction of greater magnitude on the part of the other. From the standpoint of the first side, this counteraction legitimatizes the action it took in the first place. Its prophesy is fulfilled. The cycle has run its course, a new one of increased magnitude is begun. Demands are for stronger and more aggressive action in the next cycle—meeting aggression with aggression is the only alternative to defeat.

Forces Acting Against a Posture of Problem Solving

The difficulty of breaking away from the assumption that *disagreement is inevitable* can be seen in the following consideration. What if a member on either side in such an intergroup win-lose conflict were to confront his fellow members with other than support? That is, what if he were to challenge them to examine their own conduct? The likelihood is that he would be seen as a deviant—as a member who does not value his association. As a result, his motives would be suspected. He could be regarded as traitorous and untrust-worthy. The possible loss of membership associated with treachery, or the stigma of untrustworthiness that can be at-tached to such actions, is an extremely high personal price for attempting to bring about problem-solving. Because few are able to pay this psychological price, conditions are created that prevent anyone from breaking the myth which en-shrouds intergroup win-lose interactions.[18]

In summary, the win-lose trap is, for all practical purposes, a foolproof structure. The parties lose perspective. The capac-ity for empathy between the victor and the vanquished, seems lost. They simply cannot understand each other.

References

1. See for example, Dubin, R. "Power and Union Management Re-lations." *Admi. Sci. Q.*, 2, 1957, 60-81; Dubin, R. "A Theory of Con-flict and Power in Union-Management Relations." *Industr. Labor Relat. Rev.*, 13, 1960, 501-518; McMurray, R. "War and Peace in Labor Relations." *Harvard Bsns. Rev.*, 33, 1955, 48-60; Shostak, A. B. "Looking Around: Labor Relations." *Harvard Bsns. Rev.*, 37, (6), 1959, 25-31, 175-176; and Stagner, R. *Psychology of Industrial Con-flict.* New York: John Wiley, 1956.

2. Doherty, R. P. "Pitfalls in Collective Bargaining." American Management Association: *Gen. Mgmt. Series,* (176), 1955.

3. Miller, F. G. and Remmers, H. H. "Studies in Industrial Empa-thy. Management's Attitudes Toward Industrial Supervision and their Estimates of Labor Attitudes." *Personnel Psychol.*, 3, 1950, 33-40; Remmers, L. J. and Remmers, H. H. "Studies in Industrial Empathy. Labor Leaders' Attitudes Toward Industrial Supervision and their Esti-mates of Management's Attitudes." *Personnel Psychol.*, 2, 1949, 427-436; and Gotterer, M. "Union Reactions to Unilateral Changes in Work Measurement Procedures." *Personnel Psychol.*, 14, 1961, 433-440.

4. Blake, R. R. and Mouton, J. S. Group Dynamics—Key to Deci-sion Making. Houston: Gulf Publishing Co., 1961.

5. Strickland, L. H., Jones, E. E. and Smith W. P. "Effects of Group Support on the Evaluation of the Antagonist." *J. Abnorm. Soc. Psychol.*, 61, (1), 1960, 73-81.

6. Avigdor, R. "The Development of Stereotypes as a Result of Group Interaction." *Doctorate Dissertation,* New York University, 1962.

7. Muench, G. A. "A Clinical Psychologist's Treatment of Labor-Management Conflicts." *Personnel Psychol.*, 12, (8), Summer, 1960, 165-172; and Muench, G. A. "A Clinical Psychologist's Treatment of Labor-Management Conflicts; A Four-year Study." *J. Human Psychol.*, 3, (1), Spring, 1963, 92-97.

8. Williams, W. "Top Union Leaders are Losing Touch with Rank and File." *Factory Mgmt. & Maintenance,* 1952, 91-92.

9. Blake, R. R. and Mouton, J. S. "Comprehension of Points of Communality in Competing Solutions." *Sociometry,* 25, (1), 1962, 56-63; Blake, R. R. and Mouton, J. S. "Overevaluation of Own Group's Product in Intergroup Competition." *J. Abnorm. Soc. Psychol.*, 64, (3), 1962, 237-238; Blake, R. R. and Mouton, J. S. "The Influence of Competitively Vested Interests on Judgment." *J. Confl. Resolut.*, 6, 1962, 149-153; Blake, R. R. and Mouton, J. S. "Influence of Partially Vested Interests on Judgment." *J. Abnorm. Soc. Psychol.*, 66, (3), 1963, 276-278; Vroom, V. H. "The Effects of Attitudes on Perception of Organizational Goals." *Human Relat.*, 13, (3), 1960, 229-240; and Walker, K. F. "Executives' and Union Leaders' Perceptions of Each Other's Attitudes to Industrial Relations. The Influence of Stereotypes." *Human Relat.*, 15, (3), 1962, 183-196.

10. Blake, R. R., Mouton, J. S. and Sloma, R. L. "The Union-Management Intergroup Laboratory: A New Strategy for Resolving Intergroup Conflict," 1964 (see Appendix, this book); and Syler, J. A., "Diagnosing Interdepartmental Conflict." *Harvard Bsns. Rev.,* Sept-Oct., 1963.

11. Crook, W. H. *The General Strike: A Study of Labor's Trade Weapon in Theory and Practice.* Chapel Hill, N. C.: University of North Carolina Press, 1931; Mangum, G. L., "Taming Wildcat Strikes." *Harvard Bsns. Rev.,* 38, 1960, 88-96; and Ross, A. M. and Hartman, P. T., *Changing Patterns of Industrial Conflict.* Institute of Industrial Relations, University of California. New York: John Wiley, 1960.

12. Dalton, M. "Conflicts Between Staff and Line Managerial Officers." *Amer. Sociol. Rev.,* 15, 1950, 342-351; and Stagner, R. "The Politics of Management: A Review of Dalton's *Men Who Manage.*" *J. Confl. Resolut.* 5, (2), 1961, 206-211.

13. White, H. "Management Conflict and Sociometric Structure." *Amer. Sociol. Rev.,* 67, (2), 1961, 185-199.

14. Crozier, M. "Human Relations at the Management Level in a Bureaucratic System of Organization. *Human Organization,* 20, (2), 1961, 51-64; Litwak, E. "Models of Bureaucracy Which Permit Conflict." *Amer. J. Sociol.,* 67, (2), 1961, 177-184; March, J. G. and Simon, H. A. *Organizations.* New York: John Wiley, 1958; and Thompson, V. A. "Hierarchy, Specialization and Organizational Conflict." *Admin. Sci. Q.,* 5, 1961, 485-521.

15. Blake, R. R. and Mouton, J. S. *The Managerial Grid.* Houston: Gulf Publishing Co., 1964; and Dearden, J. "The Case of the Disputing Divisions." *Harvard Bsns. Rev.,* May-June, 1964, 158-159, 167-178.

16. Blake, R. R. and Mouton, J. S. "Reactions to Intergroup Competition Under Win-Lose Conditions." *Mgmt. Sci.,* 7, (4), 1961, 420-435; Blake, R. R., Mouton, J. S. and Sloma, R. L., *op. cit.;* and Haire, M. "Role Perception in Labor-Management Relations: An Experimental Approach." *Indust. & Labor Relat. Rev.,* 82, (2), 1955, 204-216.

17. Boulding, K. E. *Conflict and Defense.* New York: Harper & Bros., 1962.

18. Blake, R. R. and Mouton, J. S., *Group Dynamics—Key to Decision Making, op. cit.;* Blake, R. R. "Psychology and the Crisis of Statesmanship." *Amer. Psychologist,* 14, 1959, 87-94.

4

Using Third-Party Judgment
To Resolve Intergroup Disputes

Because of the intensity of human emotions associated with intergroup disagreement under win-lose conditions, mechanisms have had to be devised for shortening the period of conflict, and for bringing about some kind of resolution. Where conditions of locked disagreement exist, then, means for determining which side is "right"—for bringing about victory and defeat—have been developed. In turn, once impasse and deadlock are reached, but when both parties feel resolution is necessary, the parties may be more willing to take a chance on victory or defeat through employing some mechanism to obtain a clear decision.[1]

Assumptions Behind Third-Party Resolutions

Conditions for a third-party resolution exist when two disagreeing parties have reached an impasse, and it is assumed that no further interaction can produce a change in the disagreement. The parties do not truly anticipate that a third-party judgment will provide a path to mutual agreement.

50

They only hope that, somehow or other, arbitration will put an end to their immediate struggle. *It is from a desire to end the struggle that the parties appeal to third-party judgment,* rather than from a belief that such action will provide a path to mutual agreement.

In resorting to third-party judgment, it is recognized that one of the parties may have to shift its mode of operation as a result of the ruling. But the risk involved here becomes less objectionable than the dangers of protracted disagreement. This does not mean that the previously existing conflict remains inevitable after a third-party ruling. It does mean, however, that *one of the contending groups* likely will have to shift its operations to bring them into line with the ruling. In this sense, victory for one and defeat of the other is almost inevitable.

Results of Third-Party Judgments Under Experimental Intergroup Conditions

Further insight into the psychological aspects of third-party judgment can be gained by referring to the same intergroup competition experiments in Chapter 2.

The use of arbitrators. When negotiations by representatives failed in the intergroup experiments, arbitrators were brought in to break the deadlock and to decide the winner. The situation changed from a deadlock relationship between the two representatives to a powerless situation.[1] The arbitrators at this point had the power to reach a decision. The two groups relinquished all power over the outcome.

Since arbitrators hold membership in neither of the competing groups, they can be fair. The Supreme Court and federal and state legal systems are all based on gaining resolution through the use of neutrals. Because of the arbitrators

outside position, contestants are expected to accept the outcome as impartial.

Victory through third-party resolution. When the arbitrator
renders a verdict favoring a group's position, two things are
evident. The arbitrator is experienced as being fair and unbiased because the judgment he proclaims "only proves that
we were right in the first place." He is experienced as being
a good arbitrator because he sees the situation as members
themselves see it. "If there were any doubt in our minds before, his ruling eliminated it; now we know we're right."

Resolutions attained in this manner have administrative
consequences since the arbitrator's decision is reinforced by
sanctions. To those who lose, the resolution retains an arbitrary, mechanical quality. Losers comply because the ground
rules require it, but they remain unconvinced.

By comparison with a group representative, a third-party
judge is not gripped in a conflict-of-interest situation. Yet
those who are defeated suspect the arbitrator as much as they
would the representative who goes against his group. The in-
herent difficulty is that the arbitrator's decision may carry
little force in comparison with the strength of the group's
commitment to its position. The defeated frequently are not
moved to alter their stand.

The following remarks are reactions toward an arbitrator
from those defeated in an experimental situation by his decision.

"The arbitrator is biased, unfair and incompetent. He has
no grasp of the problem . . . he does not possess the intelligence
prerequisite to be fair and unbiased . . . he doesn't seem to
know too much about the subject . . . he didn't take enough
time."[3]

In other words, when members are committed to a position, and a third party decides against it, either the group is
wrong or the arbitrator is wrong. *In their initial reactions,*

group members have little doubt about who is wrong—*it is the arbitrator.* Results from other observations suggest that the stronger the commitment of a group to its solution, the more relevant the problem to the life of the group, and the more cohesive the group, then the greater the negative reactions towards the arbitrator whose decision defeats them. Even though obligated to accept the verdict, attitudes generally remain consistent with the prior convictions.

Delayed ingroup reactions to third-party defeat. When intergroup competition has been generated for study under experimental laboratory conditions, with resolution of the conflict placed in the hands of an arbitrator, a delayed reaction of considerable importance has been noted among members of defeated groups.

Though the initial reaction in the defeated group toward the arbitrator is, "It's the *arbitrator* who is at fault," a delayed reaction among some members is, "It's *our group* which is at fault." Such a reaction usually arises among the members *who were the least committed to the group's position before the issue was submitted for arbitration, or among those who prize their membership highest.* Rather than venting their frustrations from defeat on the arbitrator, they discharge it by attacking the other members. A consequence is that the group tends to splinter, to lose its former cohesion, and to disrupt.

Variations from the basic experimental reactions produced in the intergroup experiments appear when analyzing reactions to real life arbitration. Nonetheless, there are many similarities between the two.

Win-Lose Reactions to Resolution by Third-Party Judgment

In organizational life, for example, once a third-party judge draws his conclusion and renders the decision, there is a strong likelihood that the group whose position his decision supports will feel the uplift of victory. The group whose position he defeats is likely to sense the pangs of defeat. Thus, third-party judgment usually does not diminish the parties convictions about the win-lose nature of their disagreement.

The third-party judgment case may be one in which an arbitrator makes a clear choice, for example, between the recommendations of union and the recommendations of management. The group his recommendations support develops even greater convictions for its original position. Members of the defeated group, on the other hand, may feel violated by the decision. Thus, in both the experimental work and in actual situations, members of a defeated group are likely to attribute the reason for defeat, not to the inadequacy of their position, but to the inadequacy of the judge.

Alternative Reactions to Third-Party Conflict Resolution

In previous discussion, we have been describing the roles of a third-party judge in terms of the convictions of the parties that their conflict is indeed a win-lose situation. However, it should be said that arbitrators vary greatly in their approach to arbitration.[5] One experienced arbitrator puts it this way, "The best arbitration judgments are ones that make neither group feel like winners." The expectations of clear victory and defeat on the part of the parties may not be fulfilled, depending upon the procedure used by the arbitrator.

A judge in a divorce court may take to himself the responsibility of marriage counseling to help save marriages that come before his bench. In like manner, an arbitrator may take the role of mediator, counselor, or third-party intervener. He may intervene in a way that brings about better understanding and mutual respect and, thereby, enhance the abilities of the parties to come to agreements in the future.

The Supervisor as Third-Party Judge

Common examples of resorting to third-party judgment by parties in dispute exist in the daily activities of organizations. Leaders of groups in dispute often turn to, or may be required to turn to, a common supervisor for resolving their differences.[6] As is his organizational right, the supervisor who chooses to hear cases can make a decision based on the alternatives presented to him. In making such a decision, prime consideration is the welfare of the organization.

However, when he behaves as a judge and hands down a decision in favor of one of the alternatives, a supervisor can anticipate the win-lose consequences just described for the relations between the two groups. Thus, while acting within the legitimate formal structure of the firm, a manager can create defeats and victories among those between whom unity of effort is most needed. Indeed, an unsuspecting manager who believes competition between groups for which he is responsible is good for the organization can produce the conditions that lead subordinate groups to view their *differences* as inevitable, with all the secondary consequences described in Chapter 2 as characteristic of win-lose power struggles. These differences are resolved only through the win-lose mechanism of appealing to a common supervisor for a decision. The reader, at this point, should be able to predict the consequences that can result from a rise in win-lose orientations in his organization, particularly between units where coordination of effort is essential to organization success.

More frequent than the open win-lose decisions that a supervisor hands down are the more hidden win-lose conflicts that take form in the "back alleys" of an organization. The best known example is organization politics. In almost any segment of an organization, one can see efforts on the part of some subordinates to bolster the strength of their side and to gain sympathy for the "rightness" of their positions. Numerous forms of intrigue and subterfuge to get uncommitted members of the organization to support their side is but one consequence.

In addition, there is another negative consequence of third-party management of disagreements. Consider the case where a subordinate-manager's position is rejected in favor of another manager and his group. To protect his group from a sense of defeat and to save face, the losing manager may conceal from his group important issues or facts surrounding the decision. When the decision is announced later, it is done in such a way as to appear to be either his own decision or that of his boss alone, uninfluenced by any other groups. When managers hold back information that can affect the judgments and perceptions of their subordinates, however good the reason for doing so, the result can lead to misunderstanding and breakdown of mutual confidence. These results are fertile soil for producing a further intensification of interpersonal and intergroup conflict.

SUMMARY

The emotional impact of win-lose conflict has led to devices for shortening or eliminating direct struggle between the parties. One such mechanism is the resolution of conflict through the neutral judgment of a third party. Although resorting to this approach can still mean loss, the risk is often preferred to lengthy and costly drawn-out battles.

The disadvantage is that once a third-party decision is made, a victor and a vanquished are created. The result, then, is that win-lose barriers to cooperative group efforts are erected. In the final analysis, the parties might have been just as well (or bad) off had they fought it out. The group defeated by the arbitrator's decision may feel cheated and resentful. Only the winning group feels highly committed to live by the third party's judgment.

References

1. Coser, L. A. "The Termination of Conflict." *J. Confl. Resolut.,* 5, (4), 1961, 347-353.

2. Blake, R. R. and Mouton, J. S. *Group Dynamics—Key to Decision Making.* Houston: Gulf Publishing Co., 1961; and, Blake, R. R., Mouton, J. S. and Sloma, R. L. "The Union-Management Intergroup Laboratory: A New Strategy for Resolving Intergroup Conflict." 1964 (see Appendix, this book).

3. *Ibid.*

4. *Ibid.*

5. Landsberger, H. A. "Interaction Process Analysis of Professional Behavior. A Study of Labor Mediators in Twelve Labor Management Disputes." *Amer. Sociol. Rev.,* 20, 1955, 566-575.

6. Blake, R. R. and Mouton, J. S. *The Managerial Grid.* Houston: Gulf Publishing Co., 1964 (see especially Chapter 6).

5

Fate

A third alternative for relieving intergroup conflict when disagreement is regarded as inevitable, but where resolution is compelling, involves mechanisms of *fate*.

A win-lose power struggle can provide resolution through the direct action of one group on the other in a victory-defeat sense.[1] However, there are circumstances where fighting-it-out is neither possible nor permissible. When the continuation of a win-lose tug-of-war is more costly than its resolution, and agreement remains impossible, the warring parties, in desperation, turn toward new mechanisms. One such mechanism as discussed in Chapter 3 is third-party judgment.

Certain conditions may arise, however, when groups are locked in irresolvable conflict that prevent resolution either through direct confrontation or through the action of a third party. For example, in the absence of compulsory arbitration, an arbitrator may be acceptable to one party but not to the other. In the case of a union-management deadlock, the contract may not provide for arbitration and neither side may be able to agree on the use of a third party. In these and similar situations where conflict becomes increasingly repugnant, groups may turn to the operation of a purely mechanical technique of decision-making. Flipping a coin is the classical example.

At first glance, it might appear that industrial decisions are not often made by tossing a coin. Indeed, it is rare for industrial decisions to be resolved by placing the issue in the "laps of the gods." That is, actually tossing a coin or other mechanical ways for arriving at a decision are seldom used.

But they do occur as the following example will illustrate. In a large corporation, a meeting at the presidential level was about to take place. At the time, the Vice President of sales had the option of making or of not making a report on behalf of his sales organization. However, he was strongly committed to his subordinates to give the report. In a pre-conference with the Vice President of manufacturing, who was strongly committed to blocking the report, the inevitable disagreement was present. That is, the sales VP insisted on making the report. The VP of manufacturing insisted that he not make it because, as he said, "We have had no chance to preview it."

Above and beyond this disagreement, the VP of sales and the VP of manufacturing shared in common a superordinate need—to present a solid front to the President and other members of the executive committee. An initial search for alternatives revealed none. The VP of sales was adamant in insisting that the report be made. The VP of manufacturing, equally adamant, insisted that it not be made. At this point their only out involved flipping a coin. "Heads" the report would be made, the VP of manufacturing would not try to sabotage it; "tails" the report would be deferred and a preview conference arranged. In this particular case the report was not presented.

FATE AS A MECHANISM FOR SAVING FACE

The example demonstrates how continued conflict would

have been costly because of the loss of face to both executives. Continued debate, or appeal to their superior or any other more rational mechanism would have meant, or so they assumed, loss of prestige for both.

The VP of sales was able to save face in his own subordinate organization. He achieved this by indicating that he had not welched on his conviction that the report would be made, but that "time had run out." Meanwhile, in his own mind he knew that he had not capitulated to the VP of manufacturing.

Saving face, maintaining an image of unyielding strength, or keeping conflict hidden appear to be reasons for turning to an arbitrary and unintelligent means for a decision. The self-esteem of the parties is protected by the coin toss; it is not protected when the judgment is handed down from a third party.

The particular feature to be noted here is the quality of the thinking. The insertion of intelligence, even at the level of the third-party judgment, was not resorted to, but rather mechanisms of chance were preferred as the basis for relieving disagreement.

PROCRASTINATION AS A FATE MECHANISM

More common than coin-tossing, but still having the character of fate is procrastination. The group leaders delay or put off confrontation of the issue in the hope that the problem will go away or that new circumstances will resolve the issue one way or the other. This "approach" to a presently unresolvable conflict can also be regarded as a strategy of avoidance or denial; but it has the character of leaving the resolution up to fate.

The historical trend has been away from reliance upon the "gods" for making decisions. However, many decisions, which choose between polarized alternatives, do have the quality of the coin toss. The extent to which chance decisions have this character is difficult to determine since the appearance of rationality must be maintained in the organization. Hence, decisions are embellished with rational sounding explanations to point out the superiority of the one choice over the other. Many times, however, this superiority is difficult to determine objectively. As in intergroup competition, the defeated group, even after the verdict has been announced, usually feels that it still has the superior solution. So it is in actual life. It is difficult for either of the parties to say with certainty that the decision is completely rational. Especially among the defeated, a common feeling is that, in some sense, the decision was predetermined by chance.

FATE—THIRD-PARTY COMBINATION

A final aspect of the resolution of inevitable disagreement by fate mechanisms involves a mixture of arbitration with mechanical fate.[2] To illustrate, an arbitrator was called to make a decision between two irreconcilable alternatives. He left the room, studied the problems, and deliberated with himself. When he returned, he announced his decision. The decision was greeted with pleasure and satisfaction by the group whose position he accepted. It was greeted with disdain by the group whose decision he had ruled against. A short time later, the truth was learned about what the arbitrator did when he left to conduct his private self-deliberation. It was discovered that he had been unable to make up his mind and select between the two positions, so he flipped a coin.

Here is an example of arbitration combined with a mechanical method of decision-making. Although outwardly appearing to be a rational third-party decision, the decision was, in fact, based on fate.

When the real circumstances in this example were revealed to the two contending groups, it generated a most unusual set of reactions. Now the victory was taken away from the victorious, but the defeat was not taken from the defeated. In truth, *there were now two losers.* Both groups rose with hateful attitudes toward the judge who had tricked them.

Hidden decisions, based on fate, are the seeds for even greater problems whenever the truth is discovered.

SUMMARY

When win-lose struggle to a finish or third-party resolution are not appropriate for resolving disagreement, the parties may turn to the third mechanism of fate.

Purely mechanical means, such as coin flipping or drawing straws, are seldom used in industry. However, the same character of chance contained in these mechanical and irrational methods is often found in the ways parties do resolve their differences.

Under certain conditions, fate-decision may seem the only answer. But in resorting to this "out," the parties that take this route may, unwittingly, open Pandora's Box. The result is that they may find themselves confronted with problems of greater magnitude than those in the initial disagreement.

References

1. Blake, R. R. and Mouton, J. S. *Group Dynamics—Key to Decision Making.* Houston: Gulf Publishing Co., 1961; Sherif, M. and Sherif, C. W. *Groups in Harmony and Tension.* New York: Harper & Bros., 1953; Sherif, M. and Sherif, C. W. *Outline of Social Psychology* (revised). New York: Harper & Bros., 1956; and, Sherif, M., Harvey, O. J., White, B. J., Hood, W. R., and Sherif, C. W. *Intergroup Conflict and Cooperation. The Robbers Cave Experiment.* Institute of Group Relations: Norman, Oklahoma, University of Oklahoma Book Exchange, 1961.

2. Phipps, T. E., Jr. "Resolving 'hopeless' Conflicts." *J. Confl. Resolut.,* 5, (3), 1961, 274-278.

————6

Withdrawal, Isolation and Indifference in Intergroup Relations

A distinctive approach to interdependence between groups is where neither group is actively in conflict with or actively collaborating with the other. In other words, in a win-lose power struggle, groups maintain contact under "cease-fire" conditions. Each side remains entrenched in the hope that the other will tire and "throw in the towel," or the battle may continue as each works to force its position on the other. As another example, an arbitrator may seek to resolve a conflict which both parties feel is inevitable and irresolvable, but where they maintain contact as they "wait in the wings" for the judge's decision. A similar degree of contact is maintained when fate mechanisms are applied.

The same may be said when a state of peaceful coexistence is maintained, when mechanisms of splitting are used to resolve differences, or when problem-solving efforts are underway. Here again, the groups *maintain contact* as they seek some basis of agreement.[1]

"No Man's Land": The Zone of Neutrality

In Figure 1, the middle column involves the categories of *withdrawal, isolation,* and *indifference or ignorance.* Also, it depicts a different set of conditions than just outlined. The key to understanding these conditions is that the presence of interdependence between contending groups is not maintained. Rather, independence of activities is the rule.

Conflict is not Inevitable; Yet Agreement is not Possible

The underlying assumptions that produce *withdrawal, isolation,* or *indifference* are these: disagreement between groups, on the one hand, is *not* seen to be as inevitable as it is in win-lose orientations. On the other hand, neither is agreement seen to be as possible as it is under coexistence, splitting or problem-solving.

Indifference—Ignorance

At the base of the intermediate column in Figure 1 is shown a condition based upon either indifference or ignorance. Members of a group, who may be interdependent with another group, fail to see the background or the logic of their interdependence. Thus, they can see no basis for any arrangement other than separation. Failure to recognize interdependence is found in many industrial systems. An example would be decentralized groups which often, through ignorance, duplicate each other's efforts. Many times this is done without an awareness or recognition of the duplication.

Neutrality can be another circumstance of deliberate separation.[2] Under these circumstances, a group may have abandoned attempts to cooperate, or it may be avoiding competitive contact by taking a neutral position. Communication and contact with its counter group are reduced, if not entirely eliminated. In truth, however, the problems may be the reasons why the group cannot achieve its purpose. Ignorance and indifferent neutrality represent the maximum degree of passivity shown in Figure 1.

Isolation

The next degree of independence is isolation. Here, contact is reduced, and "walls" are erected, sometimes quite arbitrarily, which make interdependence unnecessary. Under these circumstances *each group can proceed according to its own definition of the problem.* There no longer is a need to receive or respond to influences exerted by the counter group.

Isolation is often found in decentralized corporations. Decentralization proceeds with the notion that plant managers, who are delegated much authority to build autonomy, will nonetheless be aware of their interdependence with the rest of the corporation. A common weakness in decentralization is, however, that the plant manager fails to recognize his interdependence with other parts of the company. He simply attempts to make his plant a "tub on its own bottom" with little acceptance of direction or recognition of necessary connections with the parent company.

Another example of isolation in industrial life is the communications barrier which is sometimes built between plants with comparable operations. Each plant wishes to exceed the others. Under these conditions, new product development within one plant which is not shared with others can aid that plant to achieve a competitive advantage. Furthermore, if it can keep the process secret, it can increase its productivity and profit. Thus, this method of isolation has distinct advantages since the reduction of contact insures that industrial secrets are not passed sideways.

The disadvantages of isolation as a method of reducing or avoiding conflict, on the other hand, are numerous. Perhaps most important is that the cultural interchange, which can be mutually stimulating and profitable in the internal activities of both groups, is lost. Gain for the plant is long-term loss to the corporation.

Another example of isolation is sometimes encountered when groups are given local option in making certain decisions. This may be done in the guise of experimentation or to achieve delegation of authority. For example, local option is often extended for solutions of internal problems. This action may be predicated on the notion that representatives of groups working in concert would find disagreement inevitable. Therefore, to avoid the inevitable disagreement and the impasse that would result, each group is extended the authority to develop and act according to its own internal standards and specifications.

There are, of course, other conditions of local option for which the extension of freedom under interdependence is entirely appropriate and consistent with the requirements of the situation. As described, however, local option is an isolating mechanism for preventing or escaping conflict which might arise under interdependent decision-making.

When groups cannot agree they often go to local option. Again, the similarity here with that of problem-solving by fate can be seen. Where groups foresee that disagreement is inevitable, they may split, each going its own way. Potential advantages of interdependence in working out and seizing the best solution are thereby lost.

The forces of isolationism and local option also can be seen in research and development laboratories where each project group insists on its own "hack shop" instead of using the central facility. The same forces are at work in training programs at the plant level. For example, the mechanical services group thinks that the training activities should be of one character; the training department has its own point of view, and, finally, the central administration has a perspective different from all the rest. What is the oft-repeated result? Representatives of the various groups convene. The problem is debated. The end result is inevitable disagreement. Under these circumstances, the choice is usually between imposition of a training program by the highest authority group or the extension of local option to each group to develop its training according to its own concepts of its problems. Here again, it should be recognized that *local option may be the best solution* for problems that are distinctive to each of the units. Just as likely though, local option may sacrifice interdependence just to achieve agreement.

Withdrawal

Repeated experiences of victory or defeat resulting from win-lose power struggles can lead to a kind of isolating or withdrawal tendency on the part of units affected. In the case of an organization which has been successful over many years, a kind of isolationism of superiority develops. Such organizations are usually characterized by traditions, procedures and attitudes which take on the characteristics of "sacred cows." They are viewed internally as the secret of the firm's success. The general attitude toward other industries or other groups is likely to be "we don't need them." In one large corporation there is an explicit policy. It is, "never become dependent on outside organizations." When new skills or technologies arise which the organization believes it does need, usually it does not enter into contractual arrangement with the outside organizations possessing the skills and technology. At least, it does not if this can be avoided. The more likely action is for the organization to incorporate the outside groups into itself. In this way the organization is able to maintain its image of autonomy and independence.

When we come to groups which have suffered numerous defeats, their reaction can be better described as withdrawal rather than as isolation. Generally, the repeatedly defeated group will limit contact with other members of the organization to those which are absolutely required by the work or to contacts directed by higher authority.

Characteristically, the internal structure of a repeatedly defeated group differs from that of the repeatedly victorious group. Because of the risk of still further defeat, contact with other parts of the organization is viewed as hazardous. Thus, one of the internal reactions of the repeatedly defeated group is to realign its power structure. The result is an authority structure which limits the freedom of members. Representation becomes important. In some cases only the group leader is permitted contact with outside persons.

Another frequent characteristic of an oft-defeated group is absence of initiative. From the viewpoint of the organization, the group is one which responds only to directives. Such groups usually picture themselves as existing to provide services, not to provide consultation or to initiate new ideas. The "staff" label is a convenient cloak in covering an impoverished attitude to independent effort.

A sense of threat dominates the group in withdrawal. Other groups which have similar or overlapping functions are avoided. In fantasies, these other groups are seen as dangerous competitors rather than as opportunities for collaboration. Usually the repeatedly defeated group is full of rumors, many of them of disaster. Subgrouping into mutually disparaging cliques often characterizes the group in withdrawal. This is, perhaps, a scape-goating reaction to the group's low prestige. Because of the power structure of industry and the persistence of staff-line concepts, repeatedly defeated groups are often found in staff services.

SUMMARY

The orientations of *withdrawal, isolation* and *indifference* are based on the assumptions that (1) disagreement is not inevitable, but (2) agreement is not possible. Under these conditions, those involved move in a direction away from interdependence—toward separation and independence.

Separation may be voluntary (withdrawal or isolation), or it may be involuntary (ignorance). In either case, separation reduces contact with other groups with whom interdependence exists and, thereby, reduces the need to achieve agreement in areas of dispute.

Life in industry among decentralized components is full of examples where, contrary to organizational purposes, the autonomous units disregard or fail to recognize the need for interdependence. Often the result is long-term loss to the corporation.

References

1. Sherif, M. and Sherif, C. W. *Outline of Social Psychology* (revised). New York: Harper & Bros., 1956.

2. Sherif, M. and Sherif, C. W. *Groups in Harmony and Tension.* New York: Harper & Bros., 1953; and, Sherif, M. and Sherif, C. W. *Outline of Social Psychology* (revised), *op. cit.*

7

Peaceful Coexistence
As a Condition of Agreement

The third major category of intergroup relations shown in Figure 1 is concerned with group relations which assume that, though disagreement is present, agreement is possible (right column). In the lower right-hand corner is identified inter-group relations under conditions of peaceful *coexistence*. The middle position in the right-hand column depicts inter-group relations which achieve agreement through splitting mechanisms. These include compromise, bargaining, and other middle-ground ways of achieving some coordination of effort. The top of the graph shows intergroup problem-solving.

The right-hand column moves upward from a passive to an active orientation in achieving intergroup cooperation. Thus, coexistence is a passive condition; splitting mechanisms represent a more active approach to achieving conditions of interdependence, and problem-solving is the most active, as it represents a direct confrontation of problems in the search for conditions of mutual understanding and collaboration.

Intergroup Relations when Agreement is Presumed to be Possible

As stated, the most passive attitude of the three positions for achieving agreement and the concern of this chapter, is the condition of *peaceful coexistence*. Under this condition, groups emphasize their commonalities and play down their differences. In a certain way, peaceful coexistence is a kind of isolation. That is to say, those goals and norms of a group which might conflict with the goals and norms of another are isolated by tacit or explicit agreement between the groups. "Tolerance" or "looking the other way" are the norms of conduct for areas of disagreement. Group objectives and norms which do not lead to disagreement (areas in which the groups have common interest) are the areas in which they collaborate. Peaceful coexistence is one of the most common arrangements among functional parts of a corporation. To operate effectively as an organization, many decisions have to be made. This implies that many conflicting points of view have to be resolved, since conflict is eternally being produced by an organization that is changing. It follows then, that if an organization claims to have no internal intergroup conflict, quite likely a state of peaceful coexistence has been achieved. The implied rule between groups in a state of peaceful coexistence, is that issues that would divide them are not debatable. Divergent points of view which might generate win-lose isolation, withdrawal, etc., are not discussed between group members.

Groups that Play Together, Stay Together

Another indicator of peaceful coexistence is the maintenance of harmony in non-work activities. Social functions such as clubs, company-sponsored picnics and dances, bowling

leagues and so forth, can contribute to harmony.[1] They are
not necessarily linked with peaceful coexistence, but they are
well known devices for maintaining harmony. Where the desire is to have groups work in harmony, sometimes peaceful
agreement is possible through contacts in which it is unnecessary to confront debatable issues. In other words, areas of common enjoyment minimize differences.

Headquarters-Field Coexistence

An example of peaceful coexistence on a headquarters-field
plane places the issue in organizational context. In one large
company, it is routine that headquarters personnel make an
annual inspection of each of the plants. There is little preparation for the inspection at the headquarters level, but there are
weeks of intensive effort at the plant. The purpose is to insure that the contact will be a success. When the inspection
takes place, it is likely to begin with a cocktail party the previous night. Wives are invited. On the next morning there is
a general discussion of trends. The following night is a final
cocktail party. The inspection is over.

To insure that the inspection will be well received, personnel at the plant conduct a dry run of everything they wish to
present to the headquarters group. The dry run is thoroughly
reviewed to locate any items which could be controversial and
disruptive of good relations. As a result, much of the material
presented shows positive trends of development and improvement over those presented the previous year. If some negative material has to be presented, full explanations are developed. Detailed presentations show that problems are being tackled in a proper manner. Anticipated success is pointed
out and the field group conveys its confidence in its ability to
overcome the "few minor problems" that exist.

As a general result, the inspection is a happy occasion for
those from headquarters. Under the conditions described, they

enjoy their associations at the plant level, and plant personnel have a definite feeling of pride and accomplishment since the headquarters people complimented them on the plant progress. Thus, we see that conditions of unequal power between groups living in peaceful coexistence require very little energy or effort by the superordinate group. However, considerable effort is required by the subordinate group to maintain harmony between itself and the one above it.

Peace at a Peer Level

An example of peaceful coexistence among peer groups is also to be found in the headquarters-field area; namely, among field units.[2] Characteristically, field units, because of their membership in the same corporation, are required to cooperate. Indeed, there are a number of areas in which they can cooperate without conflict. At the same time, field units are, in many ways, direct competitors. They compete to make the best showing to headquarters. They compete for new capital investment—often the reward for demonstrated achievement. As a result their relationships often approximate peaceful coexistence. This appearance of harmony can be observed when the representative of one field unit visits another field unit. He is given help to do whatever he wants. At the same time, many things are carefully hidden from him. Debate on issues on which the field units are in competition is studiously avoided.

In general, peaceful coexistence is adopted in intergroup relations when the price of win-lose power struggles is too great and the rewards for the appearance of collaboration too high. In most cases of which we are aware, peaceful coexistence contains large elements of sham. Rarely is it conducive to the kind of collaborative effort that can produce interdependent achievement.

Evidences of peaceful coexistence are readily available to

any member of a large organization. One needs only to consider two kinds of meetings. The first is one in which, let us say, the members of one group are discussing the characteristics of another group, which is absent. The second meeting is the same group discussing the characteristics of the other group with members of the other group present. The disparity between the things said about the other group in its absence and in its presence is a kind of index to the extent to which these groups exist in a state of peaceful coexistence.

The passive nature of peaceful coexistence perhaps explains the difficulty of mobilizing commitment to peace, in contrast to the commitment so readily generated under conditions of war. The *active* alternative to active war is problem-solving, not peace.

SUMMARY

Three orientations to intergroup disagreement assume that agreement is possible. One of these, the most passive, is peaceful *coexistence*. Under conditions of peaceful coexistence, groups in actual or potential disagreement play down differences and emphasize common interests. The rule is, "Don't fight—we have to work and live together, so let's get along."

A kind of "If-you-can't-fight-them, join-them" attitude often creeps into the camp of subordinate units. Hope is abandoned that headquarters or superior segments of the organization can be influenced. Under these conditions, the efforts of the powerless subordinate groups are directed toward co-existence in harmony. Also, peer groups within an organization often feel compelled to live in a state of peaceful coexistence with each other as well as with headquarters. Again, this is due primarily to the powerlessness of the subordinate groups. *They are required to cooperate.* Also, peer groups within an organization often feel compelled to live in a state of peaceful coexistence with each other as well as with headquarters.

Again, this is due primarily to the powerlessness of the subordinate groups. *They are required to cooperate.* Open conflict is avoided at all costs.

References

1. Blake, R. R. and Mouton, J. S. *The Managerial Grid.* Houston: Gulf Publishing Co., 1964.

2. Blake, R. R. and Mouton, J. S. Headquarters-Field Team Training for Organizational Improvement. *ASTD J.,* 16, (3), 1962, 3-11.

8

Compromise, Bargaining, and Other Forms of Splitting the Difference

In the search for conditions under which agreement is possible, one of the most common arrangements between groups of equal power takes the form of searching for an intermediate position acceptable to both parties. Agreement of this nature is sought, even though reservations and unresolved issues initially separating groups may remain.

There are many ways of splitting differences to achieve communications and decision-making between groups attempting to solve intergroup problems.[1] Compromise is one such approach; bargaining also has the quality of striking some acceptable middle position;[2] and trading and swapping fall into the same category. Splitting mechanisms are practiced by many negotiators in situations of intergroup win-lose power struggles where the effort is to convert the conflict into a situation where agreement is possible.[3]

Conditions Leading to the Splitting of Differences

Bargaining, compromise, and other forms of splitting occur frequently where the groups are bound together in a situation of necessary interdependence or where continued disagreement is more costly than partial agreement. Groups resort to these mechanisms most often when both sides must avoid total capitulation. Solutions such as withdrawal or isolation may not be available to them, and, for some reason, genuine problem-solving is unattainable. The basic assumption is that even though disagreement is present, some degree of agreement is seen to be possible. Both parties approach each other within this mental attitude.

Scarce Resources

One possible reason for not achieving sound problem-solving may be scarce resources. There may be certain commodities which are needed by each group but which may not be in sufficient supply to meet the needs of both. The splitting approach to scarce resources, therefore, differs from the win-lose approach. In the former, the groups agree to *deprive* themselves equally of the needed resource, whereas in a win-lose orientation, each group tries to capture the entire resource for itself. Although neither group loses completely under compromise, bargaining and splitting, all approaches are generally unsatisfactory in that both parties end in a state of equal deprivation. One might say the result is a partial defeat. Yet, partial defeat often is preferable to the risk of one group's being the total loser, completely deprived and the other being the victor, taking all.

Industrial life is replete with examples of splitting-the-difference approaches to conflict resolution. Under these circumstances, positions of final agreement are intermediate between the original positions taken by each side. To a very substantial degree, union-management bargaining is made practical by readiness of each party to compromise differences— to go part way but not all the whole distance—to achieve possible agreement.

Seeking Favors of Another

A traditional arrangement between groups in organizations is the concept of trading or exchanging favors. Thus, a group may agree to take a particular action which carries some cost to itself. This is only done, though, on the condition that the other group is bound by obligation to return the favor at some future time and at an equal cost. Once again, the characteristic of equal deprivation, or equal sacrifice, is the essential feature that balances equal gain.

There Need Be No Losers

The notions of balance, splitting, compromise, equal deprivation and bargaining all have a feature in common: neither party wins. Yet, neither does either party lose. A kind of fair trade is achieved.

An example of a compromise solution can be given from one firm. It was determined by top management that a 10 per cent reduction in work force was necessary. Was the decision applied according to the operational needs of the organizational components? No! A thorough examination into manpower utilization and needs might have lead to the kind of decision that would have caused some managers to feel defeated and others victorious. A study could have resulted in unequal cuts from departments. To avoid inequalities, the department managers agreed that each department would cut its force by 10 per cent. Thus, each department representative was able to report to his group that fair and equal treatment was being accorded "across the board." The managers were able to say that no one was asked to sacrifice more than anyone else.

UNION-MANAGEMENT RELATIONS: A BREEDING GROUND FOR BARGAINING AND COMPROMISE

A typical example of a splitting the difference in union-management relations can be seen in the following example. The contract had terminated in a particular plant, and the new union wage demand was unacceptable to management. At the time contract bargaining got under way there was no discussion about retroactivity of the wage agreement. Four months later, when no contract was in force, the wage agreement was finally settled. But, to avoid disturbing a very delicate balance in bargaining relations, neither side introduced retroactivity into the discussion. Then came the issue of the effective date of the increase. Would it be the day the contract had terminated? Would it be the day the wage agreement had been reached? Or, would it be something intermediate?

Formulated in *this* way, the problem was resolved by a joint union-management agreement. Retroactivity would be extended back to *one-half* of the interval between contract termination and the day it was signed, plus one day. Thus, management not only split the difference, it also tipped the balance away from a complete equilibrium, in favor of the union. It did not yield to the extreme of agreeing with the union that retroactivity should be 100 per cent. However, neither did management demand that the new wage proposal be effective only from the date of the wage settlement.

BARGAINING ACROSS ORGANIZATION GROUPS AT A PEER LEVEL

Another example of bargaining or trading with a split-the-difference quality took place in one management where a shift of personnel was needed. One group wanted to get rid of an inferior person and exchange him for one of superior capability. The other group, the one destined to get the inferior person, obviously had no desire to accept him as replacement for releasing a better one.

Through a set of "dickering" arrangements, it was finally concluded that an exchange could be made. But, the group receiving the inferior man was relieved of responsibility for one minor distasteful activity which previously had been its responsibility. In this particular arrangement, there was no connection between the jobs of the two men involved and the work from which one of the groups was relieved.

Splitting the Difference Between Groups of Unequal Power

Splitting the difference also can be observed in situations where groups have unequal power. A case in point was where two plants reported to the same headquarters. A technical study indicated desirability of the company's making and marketing a new product which would require a major investment in equipment. According to the economic analysis, the best approach would be to erect a major unit in one of the two plants.

On reflection by headquarters, it appeared that the placement of a major unit in one plant would result in a disturbing disequilibrium between the two. To follow this course of action would mean that one plant would become substantially more influential in the total company effort, and the other would be decreased to secondary significance. The final turn of events saw headquarters management disregard economic factors. Their compromise was that a restudy should be made as to the feasibility of constructing two units of approximately equal size—one for each plant.

The restudy was conducted. As might be expected from the original analysis, the economics were unfavorable in comparison with locating a major unit in only one plant. However, the alternative decision stood. Two smaller units—one located in each plant—were built, on the rationalization that the company would not be under so much strike threat should union relations worsen.

This is but one illustration of compromise in intergroup relations. Similar examples are found in most organizations. They often pass under the label of equal treatment, or fair treatment or even fair but firm treatment. In such cases, to avoid win-lose conditions or to prevent invidious comparison issues among subordinate groups, the superior group places equal treatment above the task requirements.

Another example of bargaining between groups of unequal power may illustrate the mental attitude of "fair treatment." A headquarters unit and a plant location were again involved. According to a headquarters' technical study of manpower requirements, it appeared that the plant could reduce its work force by approximately 25 per cent. A similar independent study *conducted by the plant* concluded that not more than 10 per cent of the wage force could be terminated without seriously disrupting production. The ensuing argument to decide which number was "right" led to no agreement as win-lose attitudes became evident.

Finally, a new dimension of the problem came under analysis. In the original plan the termination arrangements were to provide severance pay and certain benefits to those who failed to qualify for early retirement. Under the existing plan of severance benefits, the plant concluded that 10 per cent was the maximum number it could terminate. By bargaining with headquarters, the plant was able to get agreement for a more generous severance and early retirement. Then it was possible to come to an agreement that the manpower layoff should be in the neighborhood of 18 per cent, not the 25 per cent originally projected.

SPLITTING THE DIFFERENCES WITHIN ORGANIZATION UNITS

In industrial research organizations there is a continuing need for applied research. Yet, by nature of the personnel, there are a number of people who wish to engage in pure research. To make a decision that would permit some people to have pure research assignments while others would do only applied research would create conditions of invidious comparison. Status differentiation and other undesirable dimensions of differences would be created between the two groups.

One R&D organization confronted this dilemma by a decision that no one would be free to do full-time pure research. On the other hand, no member of the force would be required to do 100 per cent applied research. The point of satisfactory equilibrium finally agreed upon was in the neighborhood of 20 per cent. The "fair but equal" treatment was that 80 per cent of research time should be assigned to applied projects. Each person was free, at his own discretion, to apply as much time as he wished, up to 20 per cent, to pure research efforts. The advantage of this arrangement was that it provided everyone the opportunity for pure research. The disadvantage, of course, was that everyone concerned was forced to abide by the same mechanical rules to the detriment of the organization. The result was that highly capable and creative individuals were chained to applied work which required little or no imaginative effort, and researchers who were little more than bench technicians were expected to work, at least part time, beyond their actual qualifications. Generally, this arrangement is usually subverted by ambitious researchers. They put full time on the applied research, since the likelihood of making recognized and rewarded contributions is greater.

AN ECONOMIC CONCEPT OF BARGAINING

Bargaining is most often based on economic theory.[4] It is bargaining in the sense of economics of scarcity rather than economics of potential or economics of abundance. Bargaining at this level contains a sense of sacrifice involved with every gain. There is very little net improvement as a result of exchanges or transactions.

A Good Bargain

In some instances, the bargaining agents find the following situation: Group A desires something group B possesses, and vice versa. The conditions here are such that an exchange, when made, leaves both parties in a higher state of fulfillment than prior to bargaining. In such conditions of bargaining, agreement leads *not* to equal deprivation but to greater fulfillment of both parties.

BARGAINING AS A PESSIMISTIC CONCEPT

In general, bargaining is based on a rather gloomy philosophy. In a sense, it is a pessimistic philosophy—one that sees bargaining simply as an acceptable alternative to win-lose.

Bargaining also has a certain quality of passivity in it. Most bargaining assumes that an ideal fit between the variables cannot be achieved. Based on the "no-best answer" philosophy, bargaining or compromise results in a resolution that *fits in some respects, but fails to fit in others*. The underlying mental attitude behind bargaining, then, is that a "half-fit" is better than none.

Another way to formulate the position is shown by those managers who say there are no "right" answers to a problem.

This philosophy assumes simply a spectrum of possible but no "right" answers. This approach appears to be one designed to avoid the fallacy of the two-valued orientation. Here we mean the right-wrong, either-or orientation, characteristic of win-lose conditions where both parties think themselves to be right. Both feel they have the right answer and that the *other* group has the wrong answer. A splitting approach —compromise or bargaining—to this assumption leads to the flabby statement that there are no right answers. Admittedly, there may be better and poorer answers, but the realistic and workable solution is to find an acceptable position among the possible alternatives.[5] The search is not for the most appropriate, or the best or the most elegant solution. It merely seeks the solution that will establish some degree of equilibrium among those concerned. This kind of action may relieve some tensions but it still leaves people dissatisfied and uncommitted.

SUMMARY

A second approach to intergroup conflict, when agreement is seen to be possible, is *splitting the difference, e.g., compromise, bargaining, trading* and so forth. Here the mentality is that half of something is better than nothing.

Splitting differences is probably the most commonly practiced approach to settling disagreements. Union and management negotiations stand as classical examples. Neither side will yield completely, so agreement is possible only through concessions, swapping, and agreements to go part of the way.

The concept of splitting differences is essentially pessimistic. A hallmark of this approach is that there is no "right" or "best" answer. To be realistic, groups allow themselves to be led to agreements that only accommodate differences. Real issues are not likely to be solved.

References

1. Blake, R. R. and Mouton, J. S. *The Managerial Grid.* Houston: Gulf Publishing Co., 1964.

2. Diesing, P. "Bargaining Strategy and Union-Management Relationships." *J. Confl. Resol.,* 5, (4), 1961, 369-378; Garfield, S. and Whyte, W. F. "The Collective Bargaining Process: A Human Relations Analysis," IV. *Hum. Organization,* 10, (1), 1951, 28-32; and Harbison, F. H. and Coleman, J. R. *Goals and Strategy in Collective Bargaining.* New York: Harper & Bros., 1951.

3. Newman, L. E. "Human Values for Management Engineers." *Adv. Mgt.,* (7), 1959, 15-17.

4. Boulding, K. E. *Conflict and Defense.* New York: Harper & Bros., 1962.

5. Blake, R. R. and Mouton, J. S. *The Managerial Grid, op. cit.*

9

Mutual Problem-Solving in Intergroup Relations

We have seen that neither peaceful coexistence nor bargaining are products of positive attitudes toward effective intergroup collaboration. Instead, they are actions produced by pessimism. Peaceful coexistence or bargaining are seen as preferred alternatives to win-lose solutions, isolationism or withdrawal.

To engage in effective intergroup problem-solving, then, requires a more positive mentality. Initially, this motivation may be no more than a faith, or, at least a hypothesis on the part of the interdependent groups that both groups have the potential to achieve a better solution through collaboration.[1] The thinking is that more fruitful organizational arrangements are possible than those achieved by working independently, or on a win-lose basis, or on a bargaining basis.[2] Therefore, a pre-condition for problem-solving is a special kind of optimistic feeling toward the capacities of other groups.

Basic Characteristics of Intergroup Problem-Solving

As used in this chapter, the words *intergroup problem-solving* need to be given clear definition to distinguish this concept of resolving differences from the positions of bargaining or compromise.

The distinction is that *intergroup problem-solving emphasizes solving the problem,* not accommodating different points of view.[3] This problem-solving approach identifies the causes of reservation, doubt and misunderstandings between groups confronted with disagreement. Alternative ways of approaching conflict resolution are explored. In true problem-solving, the alternative solutions which emerge may not be ones held by either of the contending groups at the outset. In the event of a range of alternatives, one characteristic feature is for groups to test possible alternatives by such appropriate arrangements as experimental try-outs. Testing alternatives provides an indication of the quality of the solution. Wiser judgments are one result.

When contesting groups move into true problem-solving for achieving agreement, distinct features of group behavior are visible. This behavior stands in contrast to that seen in the intergroup win-lose experiments and the real-life analysis drawn from industrial win-lose conflict examples. For example, group representatives become link-pins between their groups. Understanding, confidence, trust and respect are the bases for achieving agreement and integrating group efforts. The effect is to unify interdependent groups, rather than to cast them further apart.

The Function of Superordinate Goals

True intergroup problem-solving recognizes that the problem is in the *relationship between groups.*[4] This is far different from perceiving the difficulty to be in each group *sepa-*

rately. Thus, if the problem is in the relationship, then it must be defined by those who have the relationship. Also, if solutions are to be developed, the solutions have to be generated by those who share the responsibility for seeing that the solutions work.

Emergent vs. Imposed Goals

With a problem-solving approach, genuinely significant superordinate goals frequently emerge from the joint-effort of those who are interdependent.[5] When superordinate goals of this character are developed, it then becomes possible to see the broader opportunities for and potential of cooperation. Opportunities such as these permit both groups to attain goals which are not attainable through independent action.

Consider the situation of groups in a problem-solving relation. Defensiveness and other barriers to working together are reduced. Superordinate goals have real meaning as a common guide to setting of self-objectives or to the adoption of particular routes and solutions. New and different superordinate goals, beyond those previously recognized, are likely to emerge. However, intergroup problems *are not relieved merely by the imposition of superordinate goals,* even when both groups agree that the superordinate goals are important. The relationship between the groups has to change first.

Superordinate Goal or Common Enemy?

Certain forces act on groups in ways that are similar to superordinate goals, for example, when groups share a common enemy which threatens the survival or well being of both.[6] The result is a condition akin to peaceful coexistence. Groups agree to set aside their differences for the sake of the superordinate goals. The condition under which superordinate goals will produce cooperative effort, *without resolving the intergroup relations problem,* is when the assumed *superordinate goal is really a superordinate threat.* That is to say, a common enemy that threatens both groups can lead to a cooperative attack and defense against this enemy.[7] In this circumstance, the groups put aside their own conflict until the greater enemy has been anihilated. But, the differences that were set aside earlier, return once the threat or superordinate need has been removed. In truth, then, the problem has not been solved. It has only been deferred under conditions of a more pressing need for cooperative effort. Long-term relations of integrated effort are achieved only when groups come to grips with the underlying and basic causes for their conflict and resolve them.

History is full of examples where countries with a long background of conflict have allied themselves and marshalled their efforts to repel aggressive nations. However, as soon as the threat was removed or the opponent disposed of, they returned to their previous state of conflict as old disagreements again became central.

The European Common Market is built on a superordinate need shared by the member nations. In many respects, however, this need is imposed upon the members by economic forces and the pressure of nations outside the membership. Underlying problems between the member nations have not been confronted and resolved on a mutual basis. As a result, cooperative effort waxes and wanes with the tide of shifting superordinate needs.

Criteria of Intergroup Problem Solving

One way to picture the character of solving problems of intergroup relationships is to specify some of the properties that are present in the following:

1. Both groups have a vested interest in the outcome.

2. Both are convinced they can develop final positions that represent the convictions of both.

What are some of the characteristics we would expect to be present under these conditions? Several criteria for adequate intergroup problem-solving can be specified.

Problem definition. The problem to be solved needs to be defined. In ordinary win-lose problem-solving, each group defines the problem in isolation. Facts are not explored by each from the standpoint of the other group's point of view prior to the definition. On the other hand, in effective intergroup problem-solving, the problem is not defined prior to contact. It is developed *by and through intergroup contact.* Both groups, or their representatives, *together* search out the issues that separate them. By joint effort, the problems that demand solution are identified.

The advantage of this, in comparison with other ways of approaching the problem, is that each group explores what it regards as "facts." This review, assessment and evaluation of these "facts" insures they are understood and agreed to by both sides. In taking this step toward mutual understanding, it frequently happens that the "facts" as seen by one group are vastly different from the "facts" the other group has in describing the *same set of events.* The problems separating the two groups are found through this dual exploration to be far different from the problems as defined individually by the groups.

Full problem review. A second step in effective intergroup problem-solving involves a full review of the basic definition of the problem. This step is not accomplished by subcommittees from the two groups. Rather it is accomplished through as many members of the groups as is possible.

This level of review communicates the fundamental facts and issues to all members who eventually will commit themselves to a final position. An added advantage of this phase is that it provides the opportunity for bringing up new facts. Thus, old facts can be tested against new perspectives not previously represented. In doing this, it is also possible to test the final definition of the problem to insure that it is valid—that it is a centrally perceived true problem.

Developing a range of alternatives. The next step involves the development of a range of possible alternatives for dealing with each of the previously defined and identified problems. The goal of this step is not to develop fixed positions from each side's point of view. Again, it is to work through joint committees or subgroups, so that the membership of the subgroups has the opportunity to present alternatives to each other as seen from both groups' points of view. Another aim is to understand the alternatives presented by members acting out of another group's frame of reference. This step frequently permits identification of alternatives that otherwise might not have been seen. It also insures that a range of alternatives will be investigated rather than one, or worse, only two alternatives that could propel the group into win-lose deadlock.

Debate of alternatives by the whole intergroup. The results of these debates then become the basis for reporting to the combined groups. The larger intergroup then has the opportunity to understand and to put into perspective the reasons and rationale for each alternative. Joint reporting ensures that additional alternatives which might have eluded the smaller unit are brought forward in the consultation with the larger group. If additional alternatives do emerge, they can be evaluated and placed in appropriate context.

Searching for solutions. A subsequent step might involve an exploration by the joint groups for possible solutions to each of the alternative issues. This step is not intended to rank the solutions from best to poorest. It is designed as an engineering step. The aim is to test those alternatives that seem realistic and feasible and which the groups agree upon as having some prospect of being effective.

Exploration and evaluation of solutions by the intergroup. Joint subcommittee exploration of solutions for each alternative with the *combined* intergroup constitutes another step in effective intergroup problem-solving. At this time the combined group has the opportunity to evaluate each of the proposed solutions. Each alternative is assessed on a broader base. This permits a test of whether additional solutions are possible. Combinations of solutions or new solutions previously not seen may be discovered through the rich interchange possible in a large intergroup discussion.

Weighing alternative solutions. Another step in intergroup problem-solving involves the effort of the entire intergroup unit. The members rank the tested solutions in a sequence from better to poorer. Sometimes this can be done quickly. If the earlier work has been completed satisfactorily, the value and appropriateness of the various solutions is more easily discernible. However, difficulties may arise at this point. It may be desirable for the joint subcommittees to undertake the ranking so that each solution and its possible advantages and limitations can be explored in depth. If this step is taken, then the ranked solutions are returned to the combined intergroup for review, discussion and selection. The solution that seems best in the light of all facts and events can then be sifted from the rankings.

This brief outline is only one of several possibilities for achieving effective intergroup problem solving. The important feature of this sequence, however, is that the *joint* subgroups define the problem, search for alternative solutions, and evaluate each possible solution for the problems identified. In contrast, the common approach is to *retain* group boundaries where each group does its own work privately and separately from the group with whom it eventually must find agreement.

When the joint group step is taken, conditions produce facts, not misunderstandings, to serve as the basis for finding a solution. Omission of such joint effort invariably leads to the use of power or compromise. Dysfunctional approaches to intergroup relations are applied when two independent positions are developed from a full set of *different* circumstances. The inevitable result is that the two viewpoints are understood only partially by both of the groups since neither has the opportunity to assess fully the thinking or the reasons behind the other group's analysis.

PROBLEM SOLVING IN AN OUTGOING INDUSTRIAL SITUATION

An actual industrial example may serve to illustrate how the sequence just discussed can be applied to industrial life. The example situation is taken from a sales division in the marketing arm of a chemical operation at the plant level.

The intergroup problem began when the sales division submitted to the operations division a description of its needs for the year ahead. The description included an indication of the volumes of various products required, and the prices expected for these products at each volume level, in addition to many other technical details. When these specifications were received in the production division, it quickly provoked attitudes of intergroup animosity. Many demands were regarded as unrealistic by those who were acquainted with capacity limitations, the availability of raw stock, and other relevant details of production.

Initiation of a Problem-Solving Sequence

Rather than returning the specifications to the sales division (as is often done in similar situations) indicating where production could meet sales requirements and where it could not, a meeting was arranged between the representatives of the two groups. The policy-making members of the managements of both divisions came together to review the document. This review soon established in *everyone's* mind that many facts of production had not been considered adequately in developing the sales schedule.

Identification of Basic Issues Confronting the Group

Joint task. At this point, it was decided that a joint subcommittee composed of members of both sales and production, should review the entire document. Beyond this the two groups set for themselves a more fundamental task. This task was to define the basic problems currently confronting the sales division in its effort to market in volume at a profit and the production division's problem of producing a variety of products at low unit costs. This was seen as necessary preparatory work for the final outcome— namely, developing a new set of specifications agreeable to both sides.

Review and analysis. Once the problem was defined, the intergroup reconvened. This reconvening of the two groups served as the basis for a thorough review and analysis of what was realistic and possible. Relevant issues were introduced and debated both from the standpoint of sales and from the standpoint of production. The basic aim, then, was to initiate action that would integrate sales and production efforts.

Determining an Intergroup Course of Action

After the analysis by the two groups, a new joint subcommittee was established to develop a range of alternative possibilities. These were to be ones that would meet the opportunities of the market place, and yet would be consistent with the capabilities and limitations of production.

Analyzing alternatives. The alternatives that emerged through this joint determination were returned to the sales-marketing intergroup for discussion and analysis. Recommendations, suggestions and modifications were developed on an intergroup basis.

Sales operations testing of alternatives. Another joint subcommittee was established to test the alternative solutions. The sequence continued. The solutions were evaluated and assessed in the joint intergroup meeting. Because of the prior groundwork, the preference for each of the solutions was apparent immediately. It was possible, with little need for debate, to rank the approaches from the most to the least appropriate. The most desirable solutions in each of the several areas were quickly agreed upon. These joint decisions served as the basis for the sales and production operation efforts the following year.

A comment at this point is significant. A number of the solutions produced by this method were regarded as unique and original. These solutions had not been in the minds of members of either group in the development of the original set of specifications. In other words, *conflict under problem-solving conditions had been the key to creative and innovative thinking.*

The Motivating Force of Mutually-Developed Superordinate Goals

Without coordination of effort for the attainment of superordinate goals, unified effort is difficult, if not impossible. The example concerning intergroup problem-solving between a sales and production organization illustrates this point. Prior to the intergroup problem-solving, the attitude in the production organization was, "It's *our* job (goal) to produce it and that's where it ends. *They* have the responsibility for marketing the product. The sales organization had the attitude, "It's our job (goal) to market it and, therefore, they should produce it according to our specification. We know the customers."

Once intergroup problem-solving got under way, however, the superordinate goal that emerged was the total process that connected production to distribution. The production organization's conviction shifted to, "Indeed it is our job to produce it, but in production we need to make products which are consistent with market opportunities in the distribution organization." The sales organization's attitude became, "We need to make it possible for the production arm to know market requirements. This will permit them to adjust their production effort to the sales opportunity."

What the two groups were saying at the superordinate goals level was that they *shared a production-distribution problem.*

In industry, perhaps with the exception of union-management relations, it is relatively rare to find a state of all out win-lose power struggle between two groups, like manufacturing and sales. They are obliged to live in something like peaceful coexistence. They do, in fact, have a common enemy: the boss of both. High organizational levels enforce a state of at least antagonistic cooperation between low levels. However, the mere presence of a superior who does not tolerate open power struggle does not insure that the groups will work toward superordinate goals. The superior is much more like the common threat that holds both together.

Least Common Denominator Agreement

There is a concern frequently expressed in the evaluation of the intergroup problem-solving approach. It is, "In view of natural intergroup competitiveness, is it not likely that the common goals that emerge represent the least common denominator areas of agreement between both groups?"

This question is important. Some insight into the degree of accuracy of this concern is available.

Fixed vs. Fluid Group Negotiations

Using the same intergroup sequences described in experimental laboratory conditions in an earlier chapter, groups worked under autonomous conditions to study a problem— each from its own point of view. In this way differences in position were established.

Fixed negotiation. Rather than pinpointing its position to a single point of view, each group was instructed to develop its position as a series of alternatives. Then the representative of each group was instructed that when interacting with the representative of the other group, he should try to get his set of alternatives adopted. This is called *fixed negotiation.*

Fluid negotiations. Under other circumstances, the same instructions were given to groups with regard to developing a series of alternatives. During negotiations, however, the representative was freed by his group to work *with* the representative of the other group; that is, to come up with the best ranking of alternatives. He was not instructed to get his set of alternatives adopted, but rather, to interact with the representative of the other group in such a way as to come up with the *single best ranking.*

Comparison of the results of these two conditions leads to the following conclusion. As judged by independent experts, the fluid negotiations resulted in the best alternatives from each of the groups. In addition, there emerged a range of new and creative alternatives. These alternatives had not been in the rankings of either of the autonomous groups prior to intergroup-problem solving.

The conclusion, then, is that in fluid intergroup problem-solving efforts, there is no least common denominator agreement. Rather, trivial or unimportant items are eliminated and the important items are kept. Under the fluid condition where objective judgment is possible, the best alternatives from each group's positions find their way into the intergroup problem-solving. An additional product is that alternatives are highly creative.

SUMMARY

The preceding chapters have provided a framework for analyzing difficulties and opportunities in intergroup relations. Solutions predicated on the assumption that disagreement is inevitable are pessimistic. In the final analysis, they leave intergroup relations in a static state. The basic problem of cooperation remains unresolved.

Solutions in the middle category hold that disagreement is not inevitable but that agreement is impossible. These solutions are equally pessimistic. The best they can contribute is a breaking of contact between groups which have the fundamental need to achieve coordination and interdependence of efforts.

The solutions in the right hand column are predicated on the assumption that an agreement is possible. This orientation is more optimistic. It does not disregard the possibility that some common values can be achieved through intergroup interdependence.

Within this framework of solutions, peaceful coexistence smooths over the problem. In many respects, the peaceful coexistence condition also is pessimistic. Essentially, it says the only place we can find areas of agreement is where we already know we agree. In areas where we have not yet achieved agreement, there is no point in trying. The best arrangement is to keep them out of the relationship. A subassumption of peaceful coexistence is that fighting is destructive. Hence the only alternative the parties have is to cooperate in areas where they have no reason to fight—where there are no antagonisms. The disadvantage is that the areas in which there are antagonisms are the very ones that need to be resolved.

The method that searches for compromises and middle ground positions provides a basis for some kind of a coordination, imperfect though compromises and middle ground splits may be.

In summary then, these eight orientations are pessimisitc. Even compromise and bargaining do not imply that more can be expected than splitting of what the two parties bring to it. There is no optimism that the parties together can create a better solution than either of them already has. The parties share little hope that together they can develop a richer life.

The genuinely sound solution as we see it is in the

intergroup problem-solving described in this chapter. If intergroup problem-solving can be achieved then each group is in a position to retain its autonomy. At the same time, each is able to make its full contribution to the goals they share in common.

The attainment of intergroup problem-solving is by no means an easy task. It requires application of the highest caliber of managerial skills.

The fundamental question at this point is, "By what means is it possible to shift an intergroup relationship which is in one of the other eight states of interdependence to a condition of true problem-solving?"

There are two quite different answers to this basic question. One answer involves a series of ways of trying to intervene in the lives of both groups in such a way as to induce problem-solving that is administrative and legal. The other basic approach involves educational intervention. In the following chapters we will examine both types of intervention.

References

1. Blake, R. R. and Mouton, J. S. *Group Dynamics—Key to Decision Making.* Houston: Gulf Publishing Co., 1961.

2. Blake, R. R. and Mouton, J. S. *The Managerial Grid.* Houston: Gulf Publishing Co., 1964.

3. Katz, D. "Consistent Reactive Participation of Group Members and Reduction of Intergroup Conflict." *J. Confl. Resol.,* 3, (1), 1959, 28-40.

4. Sherif, M. "Superordinate Goals in the Reduction of Intergroup Conflict." *Am. J. Soc.,* 43, 1958, 349-356; and, Sherif, M. and Sherif, C. W. *Outline of Social Psychology* (revised). New York: Harper & Bros., 1956.

5. Blake, R. R. and Mouton, J. S. *The Managerial Grid, op. cit.*

6. Sherif, M. and Sherif, C. *Outline of Social Psychology* (revised), *op. cit.*

7. Roy, D. "Efficiency and 'the Fix'; Informal Intergroup Relations in a Piece-Work Machine Shop." *Am. J. Soc.,* 60, 1954, 255-266.

———*10*

Intervention into Situations of Intergroup Conflict

Various methods have become traditional for governing of intergroup relations. The methods used by persons or groups in intergroup relations correspond with their location in any one of the nine positions specified in Figure 1.

METHODS OF INTERVENTION

The question to be dealt with here is what kind of intervention might be made under each of the three basic sets of assumptions shown in Figure 1.

1. Conflict is inevitable and agreement is impossible (first column).

2. Conflict is not inevitable, yet agreement is not possible (second column).

3. Although conflict may exist, agreement is possible (third column).

Intervention when Conflict Is Inevitable; Agreement Is Impossible

Intervention by fate mechanisms. Where disagreement is seen to be inevitable, fate is one method for deciding a winner. What would be the strategy of implementing this method of win-lose resolution? One may be to appeal to the "sportsmanship" of the group. Or, the intervener may serve as referee to insure that the parties, once having adopted a system for deciding who will be winner, play by the "rules of that game."

One company for example, invested in new plant equipment in order to manufacture new products. However, it would have been just as appropriate to have added this new investment to any of the other plants of the corporation. There was essentially no basis for choosing among them in terms of economic advantage, technological capacity, nearness to market, raw materials, or energy. Therefore, the choice was an arbitrary one. The decision was made in a manner quite similar in character to flipping a coin.

In announcing the location for the new investment, the Vice President of manufacturing put out an "appropriate" memorandum. In his memorandum, he expressed a desire that the plant managers, who were denied the new investment, accept the decision in a "sportsmanlike" way.

Third-party intervention. Moving up the first vertical column in Figure 1 to the third party judgment position under which the stakes are higher, the question becomes, "What recommendations would be made by one who recommends third-party judgment?" It can be expected that at least two approaches might arise under these circumstances. One is that he would recommend that the power of the third party be greater than that of the combined groups. This would insure that judgment is final and complete. The second thing is that the scope of the *third party's authority be increased.* For example, arbitration would be made compulsory rather than voluntary. Subordinates would be required to bring all disagreements to their superiors for judgment.

Out of this, then, emerges the concept of a static authority structure; a permanent institutionalized means of resorting to arbitration or, let us say, to the imposition of superior judgment to decide winner and loser. In this sense, a very large portion of bureaucratic organization theory emerges from third-party judgment. Just as this method recommends the erection and use of an authority structure as a basis for deciding a winner and a loser, it also produces a set of governing rules and mechanisms for determining the way that industrial disputes will be handled. Enforcement of "cooling-off" periods or arbitration in cases of essential or critical industries are examples of the third-party judgment concept operating at the institutional or governmental level. The same can be said for our anti-trust laws that result in the settlement of issues in industry.

In a social system such as we have in the United States today, which relies heavily on third-party judgment for determining winner and loser, it is not surprising that the role of arbitration to resolve intergroup disputes has steadily increased over the past 50 years. Most union-management contracts today call for the use of arbitration over a far wider range of events than was true even 20 years ago.[1]

Daily decision-making processes in industry have stressed the exercise of judgment by the supervisor in making decisions. These decisions generally are based on the data and recommendations given to him by his subordinates. From the subordinates' points of view, for example, where two staff groups are recommending different courses of action to a line manager, the issue for them may well be victory or defeat. The line manager in making his decision is, in fact, also producing a verdict of win-lose between the two groups.

Intervention from a win-lose orientation. Moving up to the third position, what would be the recommendation of the person who approaches intergroup disagreement with a two-valued orientation and, therefore, sees disagreement as inevitable between the groups? More than likely, his recommended method of resolution would be to have the groups fight it out. At the action level, this intervention in intergroup conflict is to choose between the parties and then help them to develop new weapons to quickly bring the other party to its knees.

An industrial example of this would involve management's use of an expert consultant during union-management conflict. His purpose would be to advise management in ways that will insure the union's defeat. His methods, for example, might be an improved campaign of management communication, such as advertising in papers and on television. The communication would be slanted to enhance management's position. His campaign might also include improved communication with first-line supervisors. In this way the management strategy committee could keep apprised of the situation in the shops and management messages could be fed directly to the source of difficulties. Other methods might include surveillance to keep union officers under close scrutiny so that management could counteract union efforts in the win-lose dispute.

Many other well-known ways of increasing the strength of one group over its adversary are used daily. Their general substance is fraud, ruse, deceit and bluff, in addition to numerous ways of "fogging" the issues by distraction to appeal to emotions rather than to reason.

Intervention When Agreement Is Not Seen as Inevitable, but Agreement Is Seen as Impossible

In the second column of Figure 1, is the concept that disagreement is not inevitable, yet agreement is not possible.

What would be the recommendations of persons at each of the three positions?

The position of indifference and neutrality. Consider first the position of indifference and neutrality (bottom, second column). What would we expect groups with a view of indifference or ignorance to recommend under conditions of intergroup interdependence?

The aim of this thinking is to achieve effective neutrality. Thus, we can expect that these interventions would give the parties an opportunity to vent their feelings in order to reduce the emotion with which they regard other groups.[2] Catharsis and counseling, then, might be one approach recommended under this concept.[3] Recognizing that agreement is impossible, yet that disagreement is not inevitable, the solution is to *increase* the degree of existing neutrality.

How might an intervener do this? There are several ways. Probably the basic one is to show individuals how trivial the issue is. The parties are persuaded that by simply withdrawing their feelings and emotions, the conflict is no longer an issue. Some religious philosophies accomplish the same end by stressing the relative unimportance of events on earth as compared with the future after death.

Imposition of isolation. How is isolation efficiently imposed as the solution to intergroup interdependence?

An example may be taken from the field of union-management relations. In this case management wrote into the contract conditions which made meetings between itself and the union extremely difficult to arrange. This was done in two ways. One was by forcing into the contract the clause that there should be no more than a minimum number of meetings a year. Secondly, management backed this up by refusing to meet at the union's request, scheduling meetings at places and times that imposed a hardship on the union officers, and so on.

Another example of an isolation solution is decentralization in the sense in which that term is often used. Many times, decentralization really means that, by giving field organizations autonomy and decision-making rights over most of the issues that confront them, the necessity for interplant or headquarters-field contact is greatly reduced. This is frequently done in the name of sound administrative practice, management development, profit and loss control, etc. One of the clear consequences of isolation, therefore, is to reduce the necessity for facing the problems of corporate interdependence.

A third example of intervention by isolation is organizational restructuring. An example is a dispute between two departments centered around joint responsibility. Resolution by isolation in such a case is accomplished by removing all areas of joint responsibility. The total responsibility is either turned over to one department, or is redefined to eliminate interdependence between those who previously were connected in a cold, correlated manner.

In a broader sense, we find a major element of bureaucratic organization theory based on isolation. In this theory, each segment of the organization, and every individual within every segment, should have clear-cut authority and responsibility, which does not overlap with any other segment or individual. Ideally, each segment should do its own job and be evaluated independently of the performance of other segments. Interdependence is thus minimized horizontally, and a hierarchical power system has provided a clear-cut method of "resolving" conflicts between levels vertically.

The withdrawal position. The top position in the second column depicts the position representing withdrawal. It will

be recalled that this approach is aimed at reducing intergroup interdependence. What would be the intervening
recommendation for a "strategic" withdrawal?

Apparently, it would be some device for "saving face," or
for rewarding compliant withdrawal. For example, a familiar
method of dealing with persons who are bottlenecks in the
managerial system is to "put them on the shelf." However,
the manner in which this is done through strategic withdrawal
is by "kicking them upstairs" rather than demoting them.
Through this subtle process, the parties "retire" gracefully,
with fewer the wiser. Many early retirement programs have
precisely this character.

Similarly, in some companies, managements attempt to
dignify company unions which are relatively weak and in-
effectual and, therefore, are exerting little influence. To save
the union's face and to make its withdrawal comfortable,
various devices may be used. For example, the president of
the local may be asked to sit in council with the managers
periodically. Management may ask him to give speeches at
the annual company picnic. Union members sometimes are
provided with recreational facilities, and so on.

Intervention when Agreement is Seen as Possible

In the third column in Figure 1, agreement is seen as both
possible and desirable.

Peaceful coexistence. Let us examine peaceful coexistence.
Here we find many devices (some of them relatively recent)
for bringing about and maintaining peaceful coexistence.[4]
One device is propaganda. Using perhaps the principles of
the Judaic-Christian ethic in indicating that people should
live together in harmony and at peace, persuasive arguments,
sermons, and other non-aggressive doctrines are preached.
This is the mentality of "love thy neighbor." What it has
come to mean is, "Be nice to your neighbor—do not examine

the areas in which you and your neighbor have severe differences."

Another method of building or maintaining a peaceful coexistence is through personnel exchange. People from the warring groups get to know each other as individuals. For exchange individuals, being in an enemy camp in which the enemy is gracious, there is a powerful incentive to avoid areas of intergroup disagreement. As a result, courtesy begets courtesy. Also, conciliatory acts of various kinds may be demonstrated by both parties. Situations may be created in which conciliatory acts can be publicly expressed and publicly performed.

Explanation and the mechanical exchange of information are also characteristic of intergroup relations under peaceful coexistence. Thus, in headquarters-field interactions, for example, the field is careful to raise questions in polite ways while the headquarters responds with lengthy explanations and informative documents.

Many programs of employee communication characterize peaceful coexistence.[5] The development of an employee newspaper, "fireside chats" with employees, etc., may be all intended to enhance the employees' feelings of importance and belonging.

Splitting differences. Moving now to the second position on the right-hand column, the position of splitting the difference by bargaining, compromise, etc., we find the intervention emerging out of this concept to be that of mediation. Here, the mediator helps in the efficient discovery of compromise positions acceptable to both parties. The mediator, being an expert, can help parties quickly come to compromise positions.

In industry, there are mediation practices both within the management branch and within union-management relations.[6]

These practices are intended to aid in the discovery and acceptance of compromise positions as the bases for resolving disagreements.

In one company for example, a man is employed full-time at the corporate level for the sole purpose of trying to bring competing components of the organization into some reasonable alignment. His efforts are aimed at working out acceptable compromises regarding who should do what and how effort should be correlated. The instruction under which he operates is that workable solutions are to be sought. If he can find a reasonably satisfactory basis for agreement in a dispute, he has more than fulfilled his job requirements. He clearly demonstrates the extent to which he searches for intermediate positions rather than confronting major issues of difference in a head-on manner.

Another aspect of bargaining and compromise is the notion of meetings, discussions and conferences between leaders of opposing groups. Meetings of this sort often lead to the discovery of "live and let live" solutions agreeable to both parties.

The practice of management-by-committee, and the despair often expressed about this method as "the road to mediocrity," testify to the widespread reliance on compromise as the cement of organization.

Problem-solving intervention. Finally, in the problem-solving concept, we find two broad classes of intervention. They may be called the non-educational and the educational.

In the *non-educational* category, rewards and punishments are used to get the parties in disagreement to work together. The groups are reprimanded for fighting when they should be cooperating, or else various incentives are provided to reward cooperation between them. The imposition of superordinate goals also may be added to reward and punishment to give direction to the collaborative efforts required of the groups.

Thus, we find under the non-educational classification that there are conditions and practices which tend to keep groups in a state of antagonistic cooperation. An example of an antagonistic reaction to a superordinate goal can be seen in the following example. In certain types of chemical production, the measuring unit of organization efficiency is the cost per barrel of chemical throughput. This number can vary greatly depending upon the efficiency with which chemical units are operated and the manner in which mechanical services are provided. In the situation being described, the cost of a barrel of throughput was $1.00. This was considered excessive by the plant manager.

Armed with this belief, the plant manager met with the heads of chemical operations and maintenance services. He told them, "Within the next year, it will be necessary for you to find ways of getting the cost of a barrel of throughput down to 70 cents. This is your goal—it's bigger than both of you. It can't be done by the maintenance department acting under its own initiative and responsibility, and it can't be done by chemical operations alone—you must find ways of cooperation and mutual help which will result in achievement of this goal."

The reaction to this charge was an *intensification* of intergroup competition. Each group under these instructions felt that the *other* group should be the one to make a contribution through manpower reduction, elimination of unnecessary functions, more flexible practices, etc. Each group, in other words, wanted to protect its own operations. The intervention which was intended to promote cooperation actually produced more competition.

The other category of interventions emerging from problem-solving may be called *educational* interventions,[7]

Here, the basic assumption is that the parties can only work together if they can find a new culture in which to view and understand each other.[8] The assumption is that through various techniques of re-education, the perceptions and the relationships between groups can be changed in such a way as to reduce the barriers to cooperative effort, *e.g.* stereotyped thinking, misunderstanding the intentions of others, past history of hostile relationships, and so forth.[9]

Such an approach requires new concepts and a theory about problem-solving that can provide a framework for analyzing and understanding intergroup phenomena. The formulation of this issue in its full complexity, however, is outside the scope of this book, although a two-step process can be mentioned.

The two-step process of achieving fully integrated intergroup problem-solving involves first of all, developing a fundamental understanding of problems of intergroup competition and cooperation *through an educational intervention.* The second aspect relates to *learning how to apply* effective intergroup relations in an organization. This application is framed against a background of historical problems of intergroup cooperation and against experimental efforts in learning how to apply such a theory in the approach to intergroup problems.

SUMMARY

The interventions one might make to resolve intergroup conflict are based largely on assumption regarding conflict. If one assumes, for example, that conflict is inevitable and that agreement is impossible, then the method used is likely to be *fate, third-party judgment,* or *win-lose.*

Where the assumption is that conflict is not necessarily inevitable but that agreement is impossible, the methods of *neutrality, withdrawal* or *isolation* most likely will be used. On the other hand, if agreement is seen to be possible, a different set of interventions is more likely to be employed. The approach may be *peaceful coexistence* or *splitting of differences.*

A third approach could be one of mutual *problem-solving.* Under this approach, one assumes that effective collaborations can be gained only through a process based on education and applied within a systematic framework for formulating relevant issues of intergroup relations.

References

1. See for example, Drewes, D. W. and Blanchard, R. E. "A Factorial Study of Labor Arbitration Cases." *Personnel Psychol.,* 12, 1959, 303-310; Evan, W. M. "Power, Bargaining, and Law: A Preliminary Analysis of Labor Arbitration Cases." *Social Problems,* 7, 1959, 4-15; and, Stone, M. *Labor-Management Contracts at Work: Analysis of Awards Reported by the American Arbitration Association.* New York: Harper & Bros., 1961.

2. Douglas, A. "The Peaceful Settlement of Industrial and Intergroup Disputes." *J. Confl. Resolut.,* 1, 1957, 69-81; and, Selekman, B. M. "Handling Shop Grievances." *Harvard Bsns. Rev.,* 23, 1945, 469-483.

3. Blake, R. R., and Mouton, J. S. *The Managerial Grid.* Houston: Gulf Publishing Co., 1964.

4. Lundberg, G. A. "How to Live With People Who are Wrong." *Humanist,* 2, 1960, 74-84.

5. See for example Chapter 4 in Blake, R. R. and Mouton, J. S. *The Managerial Grid, op. cit.*

6. Kerr, C. "Industrial Conflict and its Mediation." *Am. J. Soc.,* 60, 1954, 230-245; McPherson, W. H. "Grievance Mediation Under Collective Bargaining." *Industrial and Labor Relations Review,* 1956, 200-212; and, Meyer, A. S. "Function of the Mediator in Collective Bargaining." *Indust. & Labor Relat. Rev.* (13) 1960, 159-165.

7. Shepard, H. A. and Blake, R. R. "Changing Behavior Through Cognitive Change." *Hum. Organization,* 21, (2), 1962, 88-96.

8. Blake, R. R., Mouton, J. S. and Sloma, R. L. *Beginning a New Organization With a Team Action Laboratory.* Dallas: Internal Rev-

enue Service, 1964; and, Blake, R. R., Mouton, J. S. and Sloma, R. L. "The Union-Management Intergroup Laboratory: A New Strategy for Resolving Intergroup Conflict." 1964, (see Appendix, this book).

9. Beckhard, R. "Helping a Group With Planned Change: A Case Study." *J. Soc. Issues,* 15, 1959, 13-19; Muench, G. A. "A Clinical Psychologist's Treatment of Labor-Management Conflicts." *Personnel Psychol.,* 12, (8), Summer, 1960, 165-172.

11

Strategies for Improving Headquarters-Field Relations

Organizations whose operations extend over great distances encounter complex problems in maintaining effective integration between the headquarters facility and field installations.[1] Geographical distance makes communications difficult. Differences in regional experience are hard for the person at a distance to comprehend. Psychological distance develops to enhance the mechanical difficulties created by geography.

In all other parts of an organization, superordinate groups are joined to subordinate groups by a common member, *i.e.,* the leader of a subordinate group is himself a subordinate in the group consisting of himself, his peers and his boss.[2] The linkpin between groups of unequal power, while more responsive to those above than below, nontheless has a powerful mediating effect. He is placed in personal conflict and stress if the two groups in which he has membership are in conflict. The stresses on the foreman are so great that in many organizations he loses membership in both groups; that is, he has little influence up or down. Clearly, there is no linkpin between union and management, and through union-

114

ization and legislative supports, union and management are approximately equal in power.

Most headquarters-field relationships lack this cement, and it is not uncommon for negative attitudes to develop between the parties. In formal theory, field units are subordinate to headquarters, but field units can acquire great informal power. This is particularly true if one field organization is very much larger than other field divisions and accounts for a majority, or at least a large portion, of the company's business. In such cases, the head of the field division may be given formal membership in the top corporate group, thus providing the missing cement. But if, as is more often the case, there are several large or many small field units, headquarters maintains its power by placing them in competition with one another. Building good relations and a good record with headquarters can lead to promotion for key executives in a field unit and to a favored position when headquarters contemplates new investment.

Field groups can develop resentment toward headquarters for many reasons. For example, each field unit is, in most companies, treated as a profit center. However, the profitability of the whole corporation may sometimes require that a given field unit do something which reduces its own profitability. Similarly, new investment by headquarters in one field unit can arouse feelings of injustice in others.

Such problems were causing severe deterioration of relationships between headquarters and a large division in the Tennex Corporation. The following pages describe the problem-solving procedures employed to bring about adequate working relationships. The design was, of course, adapted to the particular set of problems being experienced by Tennex. A different design would be used, for example, if the object were to build better team relations among several field units, and between them and headquarters.

THE SCOFIELD CASE

The following example illustrates an approach to the improvement of working relationships between headquarters and field. The Scofield division is one of several subsidiaries of the Tennex Corporation. The Tennex Corporation is a highly diversified organization, moderately decentralized.

Since World War II, Tennex has grown quite rapidly, partly by acquisition. Corporate efforts to develop strategies in marketing and production which took advantage of its diverse resources brought many changes which affected Scofield, one of the divisions. Over a period of years, a number of points of friction had developed between the division's management and the top corporate management.

Headquarters personnel felt the division managers were "secretive" and "unresponsive." The division was looked upon as unwilling to provide information that headquarters felt it needed. In turn, Scofield division management saw the headquarters management as "prying" and "arbitrary." For example, headquarters was critical of the labor relations practices of the division. The division management resented the criticism, regarding it as prejudiced and ill-informed. Again, headquarters felt that Scofield managers had been "dragging their feet" in implementing corporate marketing policies. Scofield felt that headquarters' demands in this area were unrealistic and that the corporate marketing group was behaving "unilaterally," and so on.

The behavioral science consultants called in to help first acquainted themselves with key management in both locations and were exposed to the patterns of action and reaction, frustration and negative stereotypes, which characterize a deteriorating intergroup working relationship. Some of the headquarters executives were considering replacing certain Scofield managers. The latter, in their turn, were attempting to influence other top corporate officers in Scofield's behalf.

Gaining Perspective on Intergroup and Intragroup Dynamics

In separate three-day conferences with each group, the consultants provided intragroup (or "team") and intergroup training experiences and theory. The intergroup training had two effects. First, managers were able to see the headquarters-field problem in sufficient perspective to analyze the destructive consequences of the win-lose trap which had been dictating their actions. Second, an intergroup experiment and its analysis created a degree of openness within each group of managers that enabled them to review their own intragroup relationships and to develop greater mutual understanding and acceptance. This teamwork training is an important prelude to intergroup confrontation, because friction, "politics," or inability to level within each team clouds and confuses intergroup communication when the two groups are brought together.

The Headquarters-Field Laboratory

As a next step after the separate three-day conferences, the two teams met together, again for a three-day period. It will be convenient to describe their work as a sequence of phases.

Phase I: listing issues requiring joint problem-solving. The laboratory opened with a joint session in which members discussed those issues they felt the group should debate. These were then listed in order of priority to provide an overview of the work to be accomplished over the three-day period.

Phase II: preparation of group self-images and images of the other group. Each group met separately to prepare a description of itself as viewed by its members. The issues listed in Phase I provided a basis for elaborating and giving substance to the self-image descriptions.

Next, each group constructed a verbal image *of the other group.* Scofield's "secretiveness" as experienced by headquarters and headquarters' "prying" as experienced by Scofield could thus be brought into open communication.

Finally, each group built a description of the relationship between Tennex headquarters and the Scofield division.

These images were developed to provide a background statement of existing attitudes, feelings and difficulties which needed to be examined, understood and overcome.

Phase III: exchange of images. During this phase, each group in turn exposed its own image of itself, and in turn listened to the image as perceived by the other group. The process of bringing these images into the open created a background of understanding and brought a new atmosphere of mutual acceptance into the discussion.

Finally, a review was undertaken of relationship problems with respect to the issues that had been listed at the beginning of the conference. Since most of these were related to specific functions and activities, they provided the basis for moving to the subgroup meetings of Phase IV.

Phase IV: subgroup meetings based on similarity of function in field and headquarters. During Phase IV, members from the headquarters staff with functional responsibilities at the corporate level met with Scofield managers who had responsibility for the corresponding function in the plant.

The purpose of these discussions was akin to the "team development" of the earlier three-day conferences: to explore relationship problems between individuals whose responsibilities make them interdependent. Once interpersonal relationship issues had been explored and sources of difficulty had been cleared out of the way, it was possible to discuss functional problems in a climate conducive to understanding and collaboration.

The latter part of Phase III and beginning of Phase IV brought out dramatically how confused and inadequate communication between Scofield and headquarters had been in many areas. The headquarters group seized on the relationship-image exchange as an excellent opportunity to "explain" to Scofield things that they believed Scofield did not understand. As the discussion proceeded, however, the tables were turned. When the field group presented its view of the relationship it began to "get through" to headquarters. By the end of Phase IV, headquarters staff members were *really* able to understand operational difficulties from a field point of view. They were also able to see more clearly how they might serve as consultants in the field, rather than as persons who attempt to "control" field operations.

Phase V: review and planning. In this phase the two groups met to prepare an overall summary of problems that had been identified and defined. This led to a joint discussion of the kinds of changes required to bring about improvements. Some of the problems implied changes in the behavior of only one of the groups, but most required joint implementation by functional subgroups.

The most significant product of this phase was that it provided a new concept of the way to bring about change and innovation. For instance, prior to the headquarters-field conference, it was accepted that "headquarters formulates policy; the field implements it." The inappropriateness of this concept for policies which had long been in force was evident to both parties. Reports from the field told headquarters whether the policy was being implemented adequately and enabled the headquarters to take special action where departures from policy were detected.

Conference discussions clearly disclosed that this control was woefully inadequate during a period of policy-changing, policy-making or during implementation of new or changed policies. Communication distortions and breakdowns, areas of mutual frustration, with the accompanying charges of "foot-dragging" and "arbitrariness," were seen to be the result of those methods which had been used in developing and implementing new policies.

Both sides came to see clearly that making and implementing new or changed policy is a complex process requiring continuous feedback among those involved. Efforts to implement a change are experiments, the results of which need to be quickly available to the organization. They are reality-tests which may lead to policy modification, and they are explorations to find sufficient methods of implementation. The policy-making-and-implementing process was thus seen as an innovation phase requiring open communication and collaboration among members of the leadership groups.

Phase VI: followup. By the end of Phase V, much had been accomplished in the areas of mutual trust, respect and understanding. Moreover, the groups had made a number of commitments to new ways of working, and had reached a number of agreements in defining certain problems and the courses of action to be taken in solving them.

Realizing that planning is insufficient to bring about desired results, the groups established some means for operational followup. The groups also agreed to reconvene for review and evaluation after a period of implementation. The purpose of this meeting would be to insure that they could find ways to handle possible difficulties in carrying out the plans of Phase V, and in "checking on the health" of the relationship. Thus, if new sources of friction were to arise for which no problem-solving procedure was available, they could be dealt with appropriately.

SUMMARY

The normal day-by-day working arrangements between the headquarters facilities and field units often generate many problem areas. Some of the problems tend to become chronic. As a rule, formal communication and decision-making arrangements are insufficient for correcting these chronic difficulties.

Headquarters-field training situations as described in this chapter are useful devices for exploring and improving organizational interrelationships, including: headquarters interrelations and operations, field interrelations and operations, problems at the general level between headquarters and the field, and functional and concrete operational difficulties within those segments of the organization which are responsible for smooth working arrangements between headquarters and field.

References

1. Blake, R. R. and Mouton, J. S. "Headquarters-Field Team Training for Organizational Improvement." *ASTD J.,* 16, (3), 1962, 3-11.

2. Blake, R. R. and Mouton, J. S. *The Managerial Grid.* Houston: Gulf Publishing Co., 1964; and, Likert, R. *New Patterns of Management.* New York: McGraw-Hill, 1961.

12

Problem-Solving Interventions
In Labor-Management Conflict

The purpose of this chapter is to illustrate examples of problem-solving interventions which have been employed in changing actual union-management relations from win-lose conflict to problem-solving collaboration. In the examples, the intergroup theory and problem-solving steps of the preceding chapters were basic in converting intergroup relationships from situations of win-lose conflict into ones of effective collaboration.[1]

One of the managements described here had committed itself to achieving cooperative relationships with the union. However, since there was no intervention in union efforts, the union remained adamant and oriented toward win-lose competition.

In two other situations, cooperation was the objective of both management and the union groups which had past episodes of conflict. A final example is one where there was increased collaboration against a short history of successful cooperation which followed an earlier period of warfare. In each of these companies, management recognized that continued win-lose approaches, warfare bargaining and third-party judgments with their respective unions were not sound courses to pursue. Rather, there was interest in converting conflict into cooperation.

Our examples begin with the managements of these companies turning toward a problem-solving approach in the hope of finding something of value. First steps in each setting were about the same. They involved, as the prerequisite for change, a laboratory-education phase of behavioral science theory combined with direct experience of intergroup experiments. This was followed by a study of theories for all management. After the education phase, a behavioral science consultant was available to slow down precipitous actions which were likely to lead to warfare. In this way, an examination could be made of alternatives suggested by systematic theory of intergroup conflict and cooperation.

THE LAKESIDE COMPANY: UNILATERAL MOTIVATION FOR COOPERATION

Several thousand people are employed at the Lakeside Company. It is an integrated manufacturing center where raw materials are converted into a variety of finished products. At the time, union-management relations at Lakeside had been in a state of continuous win-lose conflict over ten or twelve years. When the theory of intergroup conflict and collaboration was first introduced, both union and management felt defeated in their past relationship, but on different issues.

At the point where our example begins, at least part of management was seeking ways to establish collaborative relations with the union. At the same time, the union was stepping up preparations for warfare. The union had the clear-cut goal of victory during the next round of contract negotiations.

The first question to be examined is "What happens when one group which is dedicated to battle meets an 'adversary' which no longer acts like one?" This is the Lakeside story. The sequence of significant turning points, of win-lose dynamics in the union, and of steps toward cooperation in management, will be presented for the critical period which saw cooperation emerge against the background of conflict. The steps follow basically the same sequence as outlined in Chapter 9.

Management's Preparation for Collaboration

Preparation for collaboration on the part of management involved three critical actions.

The first step: experience human interactions and then talk systematically about them afterward. The initial step at Lakeside had been taken several years prior with the decision to engage in a laboratory training program. The curriculum focused on problems of intergroup conflict and collaboration. The critical intervention was by the behavioral scientist, whose advice was sought on how to improve union-management relations.

The recommended training program was one based on participants experiencing the interactions as the basis for systematic generalizations regarding conflict. This course was chosen over simply "telling" management about theory and experimental results through traditional lecture methods and discussion techniques. Also, it was felt that this approach was superior to merely suggesting concrete steps that management might take to accomplish its goal of improved relationships.

All members of management participated in the training program. The union was invited to take part, but it refused. The union said, "This is just another management manipulation intended to 'soften us up,' to 'brainwash' us so they can beat us in the next round. No soap."

The second step: Management consultation. The second step was for a behavioral scientist to become an observer-intervener in the activities of the company itself. His interventions were particularly powerful for two reasons. One was that he possessed the necessary background knowledge of systematic and procedural alternatives for viewing the intergroup situation and for planning constructive action. Secondly, he was not identified with particular solutions for the issues under examination and, therefore, was not involved in the win-lose dynamic.

The behavioral science interventions were made with the management bargaining team. Similar access to the union was not available. At first this one-sided relationship seemed unfortunate. However, it provided a more severe test of the possibility of shifting from competition to collaboration when access is available to only one of the factions. Intervention with one side is probably the most realistic situation from the standpoint of real life warfare situations. If one side trusts an outsider, the outsider becomes suspect in the eyes of the other. Therefore, interventions with the second group are unacceptable.

The third step: norm-setting conferences. In spite of an "intellectual" commitment to seek cooperation with the union, it was clear that the management group was still divided on this issue.

There were two polarized attitudes. On the one extreme, there were people whose dominant feeling was, "All out warfare is the way to straighten out the union and 'clean it up.' This is the only way to go. *Make them be responsible!*"

The other point of view said the opposite. "Collaborate and learn to sclve problems together. Accept the present union and its officers. From a legal point of view, we are equal. There can be no denial of that. If you accept union officers as equals, they will respond as equals. The problem is one of generating common respect and mutual trust and that can only be done if we behave toward them with respect and trust."[1]

This was a deep internal split within the management organization. It could not be resolved by mere edict from above. No one person in the management branch could, with assurance of success, compel the group to shift its mental attitudes from warfare to cooperation. The contending factions had to be brought together to thrash through their *own* positions and to find common ground.

The critical intervention at this point, then, focused on the problem of divergent attitudes and on the necessity of obtaining unanimity of attitude if possible. A number of norm-setting conferences were held.

The purpose of these conferences was to arrive at a common conviction and concrete proposals for action in response to the question, "What kinds of relations do we want to develop between the union and ourselves?" All members of management participated in the conferences. Each conference was a day and one-half long.

Many recommendations emerged from these deliberations. The outstanding one to which all agreed was, "Treat the union and its officers with dignity and respect." Many members of management did a complete flip-flop. Attitudes on the validity of warfare shifted to accepting intergroup cooperation as the only possible way to proceed over the long term.

This initial talking through was an important event in Lakeside Company's labor-management relations. It unlocked attitudes and emotions in these norm-setting conferences that released the organization to initiate a sequence of events that created sound conditions of collaboration. *Management had to develop a shared conviction at the emotional level before any steps toward collaboration could be accomplished.* The norm-setting conferences did this.

Union Prepares for Battle

What was the union doing while management was engaged in the steps just described? In the best tradition of win-lose conflict, the union was preparing for the coming battle it envisaged with management. A bird's-eye view of the events in the union will set the stage for understanding the initial contact between union and management.

The Lakeside union officers had recently won a representational battle, but only by a close margin. The same was true for intraunion election battle. Even though victorious, according to the number of votes, union officers felt morally defeated by the reduction in support.

Reestablishment of group integration in the union after moral defeat. The union needed a clear-cut, well-defined goal to permit its members to close ranks and to work together as a team. Parallel to the reactions in defeated groups under experimental conditions described in Chapter 2, the officers examined union history in an effort to avoid the mistakes that had lead to its last defeat. One mistake the union felt it had made was in not spending sufficient time developing its own positions prior to negotiations. This time, the union spent approximately six months developing new proposals to serve as the agenda during the next round of negotiations. The belligerent and aggressive tone was indicated by the items in the bargaining agenda. It contained many positions that management would find very difficult even to listen to, to say nothing of accepting.

"We are out to win"—rise in cohesion with competition. In composing its positions, the union officers and many members entered into a spirit of new competition. Even though the whistle had not blown, this group was itching to begin a new battle. By the time the proposals were completed, the union was strong, tough and disciplined. Having come to an agreement to prepare strong and defiant proposals, the union members closed ranks. The predicted rise in cohesion within a group that has the clear-cut goal of winning over its adversary was conspicuous to those who knew what was going on.

Union's Reaction to Its Own Proposal, Elevating Own Position

Union officers in their "informal" contacts with management indicated in a spontaneous way their evaluations of their own document. The gist of their feelings was, "Together, these proposals are *much* better than the old contract. They tie down many more points where management has been able to misconstrue the intention of our previous agreements. It is simple, and it can be understood."

Having "sweated through" the production of many pages of proposals, the union officers found their own product much superior to the previous contract in which they felt little or no ownership. Now, the union had *fixed* positions.

The union signals competition to management. The proposals were handed to management with a flippant, "Study them, and when you are ready to talk seriously, let us know."

A dramatic restructuring of management's attitudes also took place immediately. Even against the laboratory training and norm-setting conferences from which there emerged the conviction to "treat the union officers with dignity and respect," the deep-lying win-lose orientation to the union resurged in full strength.

Management's Initial Reactions to the Union's Proposal: Emergence of Win-Lose Dynamics

What were the initial reactions of management to the union's proposals?

Negative stereotypes serve the basis of belittling and devel oping the union's proposals. A brief study of the differences between the union demands and the existing contract was made. Differences were many. The gulf between the existing contract and the union proposals was wider than ever. Several members of the President's Policy Committee threw up their hands saying, "This proves how impossible the union is. Everyone will recognize the absurdity of the positions proposed by the union."

Negative stereotypes quickly came to the fore as members of management read through the union proposals. Management found great delight in pointing out errors of grammar, of punctuation, and of spelling which served to justify their negative attitudes toward the union. The "demands" were considered outrageous and unreasonable. They had to be rejected immediately. Management's judgments of the document, and their attitudes toward the union as a group for having prepared such a monstrous proposal, were bitter and destructive.

Meet attack with counterattack: "throw the proposals back in their faces." The dominant attitude in management was, "Let's have a meeting with the union. Let's take these proposals and push them back in their faces. We will take whatever consequences come our way, but we can't work with this kind of an impossible union." A situation of readiness for bitter conflict was in the air. In spite of earlier commitments to collaboration which had led to verbal intentions to treat the union with dignity and respect, the intense, long-standing emotional attitudes of a decade had taken over and were in full sway.

The first step in the attack was to grab the offensive away from the union. This was accomplished by creating conditions such that union officers would be under maximum pressure and frustration at not being able to meet with management. A second action was to develop a communications program that would "go directly to the people and convince them of union viciousness and of management's good intentions."

Confronting Management with the Self-fulfilling Prophecy

Management was disregarding the predictable consequences of its actions. Members of management knew, in an intellectual sense, that their spontaneous reaction of "pushing the proposals back in the union" would only intensify the conflict. Management was headed directly toward establishing a battle line to take over an entrenched enemy and force him to capitulate.

At this point the behavioral science consultant urged management to take a second look. "Wait a minute. This is flying off the handle; it is going into orbit. Examine what is going on and what the consequences would be of throwing the proposals 'back in their faces.' You are reacting to the competition urge—to the win-lose signals from the union.

A counterattack will only produce more intense and open warfare. By your own behavior, you will provoke the very fighting you want to avoid. You can't hope to receive cooperation from the union when you are in full battle dress. This would mean the end of face-to-face communications and the reopening, on the public level, of intergroup hostility. What would be the gain? Could management, on the background of its action, ever look toward cooperation, or would the lines of communication be so obliterated that no further efforts at cooperation could even be anticipated? The mandate from the norm-setting conference was 'treat the union officers with dignity and respect.' Is it either dignified or respectful to throw the proposals back in their faces?"

These remarks were enough to delay the impulse toward thoughtless action and to reset management's orientation.

During subsequent discussion the feeling arose that there was a possibility of constructive collaboration if only management could be "smart enough" to find the conditions which would shift the union thinking away from win-lose hostility toward problem-solving. Others also began to doubt their initial certainty that no problem-solving would be possible. Negative attitudes began to dissipate just slightly. Finally, the decision was made. In spite of the provocative action of "hurling a 'paper bomb' at management," efforts to establish a spirit of cooperation with the union would be taken.

Seek Similarities in Positions

There were still serious reservations about whether collaboration was feasible. One reason for viewing the situation as nearly hopeless was that in their own emphasis on differences, management had grossly exaggerated the magnitude of the issues separating the two groups.

Since there seemed to be no explicit awareness of the basic tendency to ignore similarities in competing positions, another intervention was needed. In order to break the faulty perspective created by exaggerated emphasis on perceived differences alone, the President's Policy Committee was confronted with another proposition. It should evaluate not only differences but also the similarities existing between the present contract and the union's proposals.

This suggestion produced a reduction in feelings of antagonism by management toward the union's proposals. A summary document was prepared to evaluate similarities as well as differences. In the next meeting, against this more valid perspective, management members still felt that the differences separating their own positions and those proposed by the union were too wide to be acceptable. However, they also saw that points in dispute were not so great as they had believed previously.

The result of the reappraisal of similarities as well as differences was an increased readiness on the part of management to talk with the union on a more give-and-take exploration of similarities and differences rather than in terms of win-lose dynamics. Rather than arranging a meeting with the union as an offensive maneuver, the approach to the initial bargaining session was planned in a spirit of collaboration.

These events provide a good indication of a fundamental difficulty in shifting from win-lose warfare to cooperative problem-solving. The win-lose trap is seductive, even with the firmest intention of avoiding it.

Penetrating the Union's First Proposals

Following the study of the proposals by management, the two groups came together to discuss them. At this point the approach for examining the proposals provided a basis for avoiding the reemergence of conflict.

Testing for understanding and intention. The management committee felt, with an inner degree of positiveness, that it understood completely the demands set forth by the union. They were ready to launch into a discussion centered on getting justifications from the union for what it had demanded.

At this point, another behavioral science intervention was made. It appeared that searching for justification would be interpreted by the union as an attack, and, in the spirit of the union's orientation, provoke a counterattack. In this case, the win-lose merry-go-round would begin to whirl again. To avoid such an impasse, management decided to listen to the union read and explain its proposals to insure that they understood them. The goal was to understand the problems *underlying* each proposal as well as to analyze the intention behind the words.

The union agreed to explain its proposals, line-by-line while management listened. For the first time in at least a decade, a real effort to talk, to be heard, and to listen with understanding was being made.

Reemergence of win-lose conflict. In spite of management's decision to listen for intentions, when proposals were seen to be extreme, management could not prevent itself from trying to demonstrate to the union its "unreasonableness." As items were approached, management would start asking questions in an attacking way to get justification or to "prove" to the union that its demands were unsound. The atmosphere underwent a dramatic transformation from tentative collaboration to fixed position-taking, to win-lose, to denial and counterattack. For example, after the question was put to the union by management, "How in the hell can you justify demanding this?" the tension in the situation rose dramatically. Both groups were on the launching platform waiting for the countdown to blast into orbit. If someone had pushed the button, warfare would have been under way.

In the post mortem following this session, management was tense and antagonistic. It seemed that the time for a critical intervention had occurred, but on this occasion a member of management stepped in to call attention to the behavior. It was the first instance where a member of management took responsibility for testing a present course of action against a theory that could promote a more constructive alternative for action. The strategy worked. Management returned to listening in order to comprehend the union's intentions.

Further Progress in Negotiations: Solving Problems Rather than Forcing Capitulation

After completing the reading phase, bargaining started in earnest, but by this time, foundation for collaboration had been established. The critical steps were those involved in the initial stages. Again, emotional reactions took over as efforts toward intellectual comprehension began to disappear. Again, post mortem reexamination seemed to prevent intergroup interactions from running headlong into conflict. As management acted in a cooperative way, the union began to respond in kind. This is not to say that the path was smooth, or that conflict did not erupt from time to time. On each occasion when a win-lose trap was sprung, it was either averted or overcome.

One example of the difficulties which arose occurred when a central issue of a rather complex nature, with a number of subparts and qualifying phrases, came under discussion. After preliminary exploration, a sharp cleavage appeared with respect to the economic aspects of one item. A flip into conflict resulted, with the union pushing for a resolution which would mean a bigger bite from profits. Management "dug in" and established its position, with the attitude that no more issues could be discussed until this one had been cleared up. Furthermore, the implication was that the only way it could be resolved was for the union to accept management's position.

Management took a strategy-planning caucus. During this time, the behavioral scientist intervened to point out the likely consequences of fixed position-taking. In addition, he emphasized that there were many other items in the total package which appeared to contain substantial areas of agreement. Management recognized the validity of reviewing the areas of agreement with the union as a different tack for talking through the issue of discord.

After the caucus a member of management reviewed the areas of agreement as management saw them and the step was well received. After a brief union caucus, the union spokesman summarized what the union understood the areas of agreement to be. His phrasing was essentially the same as that of management. Spirits rose. Both union and management members were able to tackle the remaining area of disagreement in a more fact-based, problem-solving atmosphere. The issue subsequently was resolved in a mutually satisfactory manner.

Summary

The interventions depicted set the stage for long-term collaboration at Lakeside. After passing the critical hurdles of establishing a posture of cooperation and achieving successful problem resolution on a joint basis, there was a healthier union-management relationship based on mutual respect and understanding. This is not to say that pathological elements of win-lose conflict did not emerge as highly important issues arose. They did, and they required the utmost skill and determination by management and union to pursue vigorously the route of collaboration. This particular situation, however, demonstrates that it is possible to generate collaboration between two groups when each stands to gain more by cooperation than by conflict, even though there has been a long history of tension and conflict.

MUTUAL MOTIVATION FOR COLLABORATION

The following three examples are from two different companies. These examples describe the different ways in which joint problem-solving proceeded, once both the union *and* management accepted cooperation rather than conflict as the basis for their relationship.

The Seashore and the Hilltop companies are, in many respects, similar to Lakeside. The same type of manufacturing operations are involved. The history of the union and management relationships has been characterized by tension and strife, though not of such bitterness as at Lakeside. Only the managements in these two companies had experienced the sequence of intergroup conflict and collaboration in laboratory training. Each had the resources of a behavioral scientist available to intervene in problem-solving during crisis periods.

The Seashore Company: Background of Conflict

The motivation for collaboration at Seashore came about because of an impasse in negotiations. The positions of the two groups appeared 180 degrees apart on many issues significant to both. The differences became frozen. No one could see the possibility of either group shifting. After several weeks of fixed positions, with both management and the union representatives attempting to extract capitulation from the other and with vituperative accusations and counter-accusations filling the air, it was finally accepted that only hopeless deadlock could result.

However, management was not willing to accept arbitration or strike. In consultation with the behavioral science consultant, they developed the following proposal in order to work more cooperatively.

Reexamining problem areas. The bargaining groups would work together to identify the problem. Committees would be set up, each composed of three members of management and four from the union for each problem area. Each committee's goal was to gather facts and to propose a series of preferred solutions to be presented to the bargaining committee in the form of recommended actions. The possibilities in this proposal for breaking through the hopeless impasse included joint problem definition, focusing on a range of solutions, increasing the base of participation and, on the management's part, attempting to demonstrate willingness to collaborate through the imbalance in number on the committee membership. In other words, if it came to voting, management could not "win."

Creating unanimity across ingroup lines. The proposal was accepted by the union. Problem areas emerged through joint definition and eventually ten committees were formed. As they began to interact, win-lose conflict immediately reemerged in each committee. The subunits of union and management "squared off" in line with their larger group affiliations. Positions became rigid. Problem-solving actions and progress went out the window.

Whenever this point was reached, the groups did not admit defeat. Rather, they stepped away to take a fresh look at the suitation. They made conscious and deliberate efforts to become fact-oriented, rather than to jump at solutions based on an ingroup point of view only. By working each subissue through to mutual satisfaction, former group lines and loyalties tended to disappear. As each point of contention was reached, the cycle of the two subgroups drawing apart before they could pull together began again. On each occasion, however, the gulf was narrowed in duration and intensity.

After three weeks, the subgroups reported back to the parent bargaining committee and spoke with a single voice.

The impressive point here is in the way members of the subcommittees drew together, not speaking out of group loyalties but rather speaking through focusing on the problems, the surrounding facts, and the most appropriate solutions as they saw them.

The ten subgroup recommendations were accepted by the negotiating group as a basis for further interaction. Whereas three weeks prior, management and union had been frozen in hopeless deadlock, the key had now turned, and the door was open for mutually satisfactory resolutions of problems. The creative thinking from the subgroups was sufficient to thaw the parent negotiating bodies.

The Hilltop Company: Background of Conflict

Management in the Hilltop Company had taken a posture of collaboration at the outset of negotiations. The union adopted the same attitude very quickly thereafter. Thus, both groups were oriented to collaboration against a background of conflict, due to the union's acceptance, at face value, that management's intentions were straightforward and positive.

Management, having learned the lesson of intergroup collaboration and the pitfalls of intergroup competition, sought to avoid win-lose traps. It remains somewhat of a puzzle as to why the union responded so quickly to a management "promise," unsupported by actual performance evidence. Nevertheless, the fact is that it did. Quickly thereafter the following events took place.

Crossgroup problem identification. The bargaining sessions for a new contract took place in a sixteen-man unit, eight from management and eight from the union. The basic strategy was to establish a number of subgroups, each consisting of two union and two management representatives. The subgroups were to investigate and to establish the facts behind each problem area. Negotiators were better able to agree on the facts *per se* since they did not have to examine the implications of these facts simultaneously in terms of solutions.

In due course, the joint subgroups reported the facts as they had agreed upon them to the total union and management bargaining team. At this point, a fascinating result was observed. In many cases, the "facts" as developed and agreed on in the subgroups were conspicuously different than the "facts" that the parent management and union groups had thought to lie behind the problems. The uniform reaction by parent committees was that the definitions of facts by subgroup investigations had produced higher quality understandings than had been possible by each group analyzing the problems separately and from its own point of view. Thus, a strong foundation was achieved for avoiding win-lose position-taking on an ingroup basis.

Searching for alternative solutions. Given mutually acceptable facts for each problem, the situation was ready for the next step—searching for solutions that would meet the needs of both union and management.

The total parent group of sixteen was divided into two subgroups of eight—four from management and four from the union. Each group, working independently of the other, used the facts previously agreed upon as the basis for searching out solutions. Of course, as new facts became evident they also were included in the basic approach. Rather than a management proposal being presented and countered with an alternative proposal (the typical approach that leads to win-lose competition), each eight-man group explored the widest possible spectrum of alternative solutions in a tentative way prior to evaluating them.

The next step was to evaluate each suggested solution as to its adequacy for satisfying the needs of each group. This led to a priority ranking of suggested solutions as well as to further revisions and refinements by incorporating desirable elements of inferior solutions.

Evaluation and cross-checking of solutions. In the final stage, the two eight-man subgroups reunited into the total parent bargaining group to compare the quality of the solutions of one group with the solutions being produced by the other. Since they were cross-group in composition, rather than being groups of management or union, they were able to evaluate solutions more objectively. Also, they were further able to modify the most agreed on suggested solutions as the basis for formal agreements.

The procedure for problem-solving between groups described here proved outstandingly successful as a basis for statesmanlike union-management problem-solving.

The Hilltop Company: Background of Collaboration

After the series of successful cooperation steps had been taken at Hilltop, a new slate of union officers was elected.

A shift in the composition of the executive board was as follows: four of the eight incumbents were returned to office and four were defeated. This personnel turnover provided the opportunity to study the evolution of relations between the same management team and a different team of union officers against the background of trust and mutual respect achieved between the management team and the old union executive group. Based on experiences of the previous union administration a proposal formed quickly in the minds of the union executive group. A significant aspect here is that this plan was the first innovative step proposed *by a union group*. It should be recalled that in each company only management had received special training. In this case, however, management had taught the union, in a sense, through its own attitudes toward innovation in the round of negotiations that recently had been completed. The proposal was for management and the union to collaborate in the following way in order to develop a bargaining agenda.

Problem identification at the grass roots level. The proposed procedure for *developing* an agenda began at the grass roots. The actual work-group units were to be involved in problem identification. First, each of the 20-odd work groups would convene for perhaps a period of a half-day, or longer if more time proved necessary. The union representative and the company supervisor would be present. In addition, the president of the union and the personnel department head, who were the respective chairmen of the union and management bargaining teams, would be included. Each of the work groups would be asked to discuss outstanding problems confronting union and management, not only concerning their particular work group but also those confronting employees and management in general. This step literally meant that the total union membership and all members of management who were in direct contact with them would be involved in the initial phase.

Evaluating and testing appropriateness of problems. On completion of the discussions, the following steps would be taken. First, those items subject to correction by the supervisor or by interaction and mutual accord between the union representative and the immediate supervisor of the work group would be selected. Problems not subject to resolution by this means would be given further study. Some would be presented to management for immediate correction under the terms of the existing contract. Others, for which there was no existing contract agreement, would serve as an agenda for bargaining. In this way, management and union, at all levels, would be in closer agreement on the issues needing bargaining.

By this method, as proposed by the union, more would be accomplished than just negotiating a new contract. Clearing up areas of difficulty not dealt with by union or management is probably of equal significance to developing a bargaining agenda through joint effort.

Continuing contact with the membership. Then, the proposal continued, as the bargaining progressed it would be feasible to return to these "grass root" groups to have small group discussions of agreements reached and of the outstanding problems remaining. This procedure would insure that employees and supervisors would be continually involved in union-management affairs.

Potential significance of involvement. Through this proposal the front line supervisor is linked into the sequence of activities that eventually culminate with a contract. He is not a passive bystander, with resulting resistive, negative attitudes, toward agreements achieved at higher levels. The involvement of both the union membership and the lower levels of management in problem-identification and later in discussing agreements as they are reached, should serve to increase day-by-day collaboration at the point where it should be strongest—the level where problems are likely to arise.

The procedure described here was accepted by management, and is now being implemented. First steps have already been taken and indications are that this cooperative sequence will, indeed, lead to a new era in effective relationships.

It should be pointed out, however, that the application of this approach has not been without its difficulties. One major stumbling block has been the first-line supervisor. Many times he feels threatened by the approach. Apparently, he fears that it will reflect negatively on his own supervision. In a number of cases this fear was justified, with the result that a new training program in effective supervision is being conducted. In all other respects the approach is working well. Its most important feature is that it is uncovering problems which have been bothersome for years, but which no one knew how to bring to a level of problem-solving.

An even more significant generalization which appears is that, too frequently, bargaining begins only after each group has: (1) defined the problem based on its own point of view, and (2) developed a fixed position, again based on its own point of view.

In several of the examples described, management and the union have learned to work *together at the level of defining the problem* and then in searching out mutually agreeable solutions.

We attach utmost importance to the generalization that the bargaining relationship should begin with problem definition, *not* with the exchange of proposals and counter proposals, as is all too frequently the strategy of bargaining at the present time.

SUMMARY

For years the approach to discord and disturbances between union and management has been primarily from the standpoint of legislative control. We think this basis for containing the conflict has about run its course, and a new approach is indispensable for increasing union and management statesmanship in problem-solving. This new approach will not come from high level union and management advisory committees or from human relations committees. Nor will it come from other mechanical strategies.

The new approach is rooted in behavorial science theory about intergroup relations. It seeks to treat symptoms of intergroup pathology in a way that is analogous to the medical treatment of illness. The orientation is based on recognizing union and management disputes as symptoms of pathology in the problem-solving area, diagnosing the causes that produce the symptoms, and treating the causes directly, rather than dealing with symptoms only.

The steps are straightforward. On the one hand, development of a comprehensive theory concerning the circumstances of intergroup conflict and cooperation is required. Needed, on the other hand, is the development of methods which permit such theory to be immediately useful to the protagonists in an intergroup dispute as a basis for cutting through their conflicts and coming to an awareness of the conditions that promote cooperation. The final step is that of guiding the transformations from theory and intelligent insight to concrete steps of problem-solving collaboration.

One conclusion is that behavioral science experimentation, concept formation, generalization, and application offers important suggestions for replacing warring relationships with cooperative conditions of interaction.[2]

References

1. Blake, R. R. and Mouton, J. S. "Intergroup Therapy." *Int. J. Soc. Psychiat.*, 8, (3), 1962; and, Blake, R. R. and Mouton, J. S. "The Intergroup Dynamics of Win-Lose Conflict and Problem-Solving Collaboration in Union-Management Relations." In M. Sherif, (ed.) *Intergroup Relations and Leadership.* New York: John Wiley, 1962, 94-140.

2. Blake, R. R., Mouton, J. S. and Sloma, R. L. "The Union-Management Intergroup Laboratory: A New Strategy for Resolving Intergroup Conflict." 1964 (see Appendix this book); Muench, G. A. "A Clinical Psychologist's Treatment of Labor-Management Conflicts." *Personnel Psychol.*, 12, (8), Summer, 1960, 165-172; and, Muench, G. A. "A Clinical Psychologist's Treatment of Labor-Management Conflicts: A Four Year Study." *J. Human. Psychol.*, 3, (1), Spring, 1963, 92-97.

13

An Intergroup Problem-Solving Approach to Mergers

A significant area of intergroup relations which is often overlooked in industry is in the acquisition of one company by another. Mergers—a primary avenue of corporate growth in America today—occur almost daily. Many such ventures prove to be successful and profitable. However, an equal or greater number are doomed to failure before the ink is dry on the final legal document.

Despite the frequency of mergers, *there appears to be no pattern or method for effecting a successful fit between the companies coming together*. Generally, it appears to be done on a trial-and-error or hit-or-miss basis. Most attempts to study or to improve mergers have been focused on legal, financial, and technical aspects. The most neglected aspect, however, is in the intricate fabric of *human* relationships that, somehow, must be rewoven if human effort between the companies is to be unified.

In this chapter, we describe briefly a problem-solving approach to mergers that has been repeated on several occasions with rewarding success.[1]

146

MERGERS: A PROBLEM OF INTERGROUP RELATIONS

Merger problems are phenomena of intergroup relations. Knowledge of the concepts and procedures for reducing problems of intergroup relations, as discussed in earlier chapters, can lead to the anticipation and prevention of barriers to successful mergers.

Essentially, the problem is this: two (or more) groups, each with its own unique culture of traditions, mores, goals, power relations, and standards of conduct, are thrown against each other. Without planned, deliberate action to the contrary, the groups, oriented toward the maintenance of their own ways of organizational life, are bound to enter into a struggle for autonomous existence. In mergers, it is the acquired group that eventually must yield when such win-lose clashes occur. This situation of loss can be devastating, not just to the merged group but also to the acquiring corporation. The truth, then, is that many mergers are consummated clumsily. The inevitable result is ill-feelings, misunderstandings, communication failures, and low morale, especially in the acquired company. Recognition of these conditions led to the development of the problem-solving sequence which will described. This approach was developed to overcome intergroup difficulties encountered in mergers.

The application of intergroup knowledge and theory to mergers requires a new focus on the problems of bringing new groups of people together. Relevant insights into group and intergroup behavior can eliminate the barriers that separate people. Included among these barriers are traditions, past practices, procedures, functional requirements and policies governing the operations of both the acquired and the acquiring company. The goal, then, is to approach mergers in such a way as to generate understanding and commitment to new ways of working and relating together.

The basic strategy of this approach is to bring *together* the groups, or their representatives, involved in the merger. This is done so that misunderstandings, doubts, reservations, misinterpretations of intentions and other barriers to effective collaboration can be explored and worked through. Once this has been accomplished, the delineation of the more technical financial and legal aspects of problem and concrete solutions are possible with greater ease and clarity.

BASIC STRATEGIES OF A PROBLEM-SOLVING MERGER LABORATORY

Exchanging Reactions

Merger laboratories typically begin with representatives of both companies (key officers and executives) meeting with behavioral scientists working with them. Each group is asked to discuss its feelings and concerns about the forthcoming merger. The representatives of the acquired group, often with some hesitation, usually begin first. Soon anxieties which have been concealed are expressed. It turns out that many "facts" which were assumed to be clear, understood and accepted, were not. This discussion between the parties generally reveals that the acquired group has underlying fears, distrust, doubts, and sometimes sullen resignation about the merger.

The representatives of the acquiring group generally are amazed at the expressed concerns which primarily center around job security, benefits, loss of identity, becoming a "number" on the larger company's roles, job expectations, and so forth.

The consequence of this first meeting, then, is that true feelings are aired. The acquiring group discovers that successful mergers are made of more than mortar and bricks or legal and financial technicalities. Understanding, trust, confidence and respect are necessary building blocks of effective group fusions.

Against this background of events, members of the acquiring group are able to understand the sometimes groundless, but sincere, fears that people have. The result is that they are better able to plan strategies for coping with these misunderstandings.

Comparison of Employee Benefits and Programs.

After the initial meeting, the acquiring group presents a detailed description of its programs of employee benefits and the policies dealing with employee activities in general. This is the next natural step since one of the primary concerns of acquired groups under perceived conditions of "threat," is focused on survival and normal existence in the new organization. This material is generally received with considerable relief once understood. Comparisons between the policies and programs of the two companies demonstrate to the acquired group how it will be affected in its new situation. In addition, questions, concerns or misinterpretations are focused and deliberated to understanding.

The rationale behind the decisions of benefits and other policies, once understood or modified and agreed to, become clear and acceptable. However, if these matters are not understood and worked out, they can become grounds for future ill feelings and resentment.

"Fishbowl" Meetings

The next step in a merger laboratory is a meeting of the key representatives of the acquiring corporation. They meet in the presence of the acquired group. During this meeting, the acquiring group discusses its plans for integrating the new company. If it is discovered that certain items have not been planned for adequately, steps for dealing with them are outlined. This thoughtful deliberation and the concern of the buyers in planning the acquisition gives the other group a sense of security.

Next, the acquired group meets before the buyers. The members discuss aspects of internal operations, pointing out possible shortcomings. When all problems of operations have been debated and related to the acquisition, the discussion turns to new functional expectations, known organizational requirements and anticipated barriers to collaborative effort. By separately talking through these issues before each other, each group gains a perspective, and understanding of the other's point of view. In this way, the orientations of the groups are guided from competitive, vested interests toward joint problem-solving. Win-lose clouds may still hover over interactions, but understanding and respect tend to form an umbrella over the parties as they approach mutually significant issues *together*.

Internal Inspection

Following the meetings, each group meets privately with a behavioral scientist. They discuss in depth their own internal problems of operations and relationships, devoting special attention to how these problems can affect the new course. Ways of improving poor relationships and operating procedures are explored so that the two groups can better integrate their efforts.

Meshing Insights and Understandings

The next block of time is split into three, more or less, equal periods. The first period is devoted to further discussions and clarification of matters still not clear from earlier discussions. The reason is that unresolved problems can become formidable barriers to effective organizational progress if unexplored grey areas still remain.

The second period is used to identify areas that can contribute to effective effort down the road. The acquired group begins to formulate those operational policies, procedures and practices unique to itself, but which could be beneficial to the acquiring company. Here the goal is not to identify and hold to cherished operations. Rather, the aim is to discover and to focus upon those operational elements which could contribute to sound organizational practices in the future.

Meanwhile, the acquiring group begins to examine those practices, procedures and informal operational schemes that could be deterrents to integrated effort. It should be said at this point that this phase is not easy for either group. Ways of operating and relating to others can become rigid and habitual. However, problem-solving orientations appeal to reason and provide objective thinking and flexible experimentation for new ways of approaching old situations. Frozen positions become areas of debate and deliberation. A result is that spontaneity and freedom in thinking and action are released to solve problems of merged, interdependent effort.

The last period is a summary by the behavioral scientists. From this summary, a discussion centers around plans for getting the information and understanding gathered during the laboratory back to the employees of the two companies. In addition, next steps for working through problems of mutual concern during subsequent phase-in periods are identified and crystallized.

SUMMARY

In this description of a merger laboratory, one feature stands out. Mergers are problems of intergroup relations.

Despite well-planned technical and legal procedures, if potential barriers to effective intergroup collaboration are not anticipated and planned for, the merger can very well end in relative failure.

A major goal of the merger laboratory, then, is to bring about commitment to new ways of working together. Another goal is to identify and find solutions to problems lodged in the clash of traditions and divergent operational practices. Overall, the goal is to move the acquired and acquiring companies toward a collaborative union through a problem-solving orientation.

References

1. Blansfield, M. G., Blake, R. R. and Mouton, J. S., "The Merger Laboratory," *Train. Directors J.*, 18, (5), 1964, 2-10.

———*14*

Overview

Life in industry winds through a complex maze of intricate group relations in such a way that it has far-reaching implications for management. Organizational survival and success depends upon how well managements understand and cope with a wide spectrum of assumptions, attitudes and orientations toward intergroup relations.

In this book, we have examined the behavior of individuals and groups in industry in terms of the group and intergroup forces that govern their relations with each other. Nine basic patterns of underlying assumptions and orientations toward conflict were examined at some length. All of these patterns of coping with conflict, to some degree, represent coming to terms with conflict. However, most are dysfunctional in that *they do not solve the problems of intergroup conflict.*

One result of inadequate conflict management is that conflict continues to thrive among groups that need to integrate their efforts. Ignoring, yielding to, accommodating or suppressing conflict are prevalent dysfunctional actions of many managements guiding the future of organizations today.

153

What we need then, is a systematic formulation of intergroup dynamics. Only then are managements better able to understand and effectively deal with the underlying sources of disagreements between groups that are linked together through interdependent needs and requirements. In this book we discussed an orientation founded on the belief that, although conflict can and does erupt between parties, there is a sound basis for achieving mutually rewarding and satisfying agreement. We call this approach *problem solving*.

It is our experience that only under conditions of genuine, joint efforts of problem-solving between contending groups is an effective, long-term relief of conflict possible. In the latter chapters we presented the strategies of problem-solving in a variety of industrial situations. Also, we have presented examples of situations between, and within, organizations where problem-solving methods of conflict resolution have been applied. Included here were situations of union-management relations, headquarters-field relations, inter-divisional and interdepartmental conflicts, and the relations of merging organizatioins. However, whatever the situation, these problem-solving strategies are aimed at bringing about conditions of effective joint effort based on mutual trust, respect and confidence. The goal of this approach is to substitute efforts designed to cut through to the malignant and festering seeds of conflict, for patchwork methods that only touch the symptomatic manifestations of intergroup tensions.

Experience has shown that a genuine problem-solving footing is most difficult to achieve. This effort challenges the very depths of managerial character and skill. But, the rewards are great. Managements, and nations for that matter, stand faced with this challenge.

Appendix 1

An Actual Case History of Resolving Intergroup Conflict In Union-Management Relations

ROBERT R. BLAKE, JANE S. MOUTON, AND
RICHARD L. SLOMA

On occasions, relations between groups become frozen, with each
group assuming that agreement is not possible, and that disagreement is inevitable. In such circumstances, conflict is the final result. No course of resolution short of capitulation by one and control by the other group seems possible.

Union and Management relations sometimes deteriorate to the
point where they are cast in this form. Under certain circumstances
the same relationships occur between headquarters and field units
within a company as well.

One of the greatest challenges confronting modern society arises
at this point. But in such relationships, must the course of events
be inevitable and lead to mutual recrimination with impasse or
worse? Are there any pathways for achieving resolution?

In this section, the Intergroup Laboratory shows how it is a
fundamental strategy for resolving such an impasse. The approach
is one which is designed to restore problem-solving relations by
cutting through the tensions and conflict existing between two
antagonistic groups. The basic design of the Intergroup Laboratory

has been tested in numerous experimental situations. The description here is a concrete example of its practice.

THE INTERNATIONAL UNION-MANAGEMENT INTERGROUP LABORATORY

The background of this Intergroup Laboratory and events preceding it are described before the actual events of the laboratory are presented.

The Setting and Events Leading to the Union-Management Laboratory

This electronics plant employs nearly 1,000 managers and more than 3,000 wage and salary personnel. It is one of several that make up the complex of a large public-owned corporation.

The wage membership is represented by several major unions.

The International union involved in this presentation is the bargaining agent for a highly specialized and skilled group, representing approximately 10 per cent of the total wage force. Membership in this local equals 95 per cent of those eligible. It has been the certified bargaining unit for 25 years and is one of two international unions representing wage personnel. The other unions are independent.

A History of Chronic Union-Management Conflict

Chronic long-term hostility typifies the relationship between management and this International local. No one seems to know how the conflict began. Little is understood about what keeps it alive and increases its intensity. Of even greater significance, just prior to the introduction of the Union-Management Laboratory, there was no inclination to seek constructive solutions by either union or managerial personnel. The assumption that disagreement was inevitable and agreement impossible typified even the day-by-day relationships. Grievances had been on a steady rise. Many arbitration cases were pending. Only the expense of pushing issues through to arbitration prevented many of the grievances from going all the way. Day-by-day frictions had become sharper and more heated. Recent contract negotiations had been characterized by accusation and counter-accusation—a full blown win-lose power struggle developed. The eventual contract represented a "no victory" result. Straight threats had become relatively common place. The union seemed to be moving in this direction in order to achieve what it regarded as its inevitable right.

How the Laboratory Came About

Several events, but one in particular, triggered the union-management laboratory.

Local plant improvement efforts. For three years, management had been engaged in intensive study and application of a Laboratory-Seminar-based organization development effort. The strategies and details of the behavioral science Laboratory-Seminar methods of organization development are presented elsewhere.[2] The significance of this is that each member of management participated in such a Laboratory-Seminar. The Laboratory-Seminar programs contained the experiments concerned with intergroup conflict and cooperation referred to earlier.[3]

In later organization improvement steps, management applied the concepts and methods for resolving conflict in the work situations. These applications brought about the restoration of problem-solving that involved friction between managerial components. In each of the applications, substantial improvement was visible. These successes encouraged management somewhat that the concepts and methods might find utility in the International union and management application.

A decision to experiment. Hardly a management meeting went by without the question of the International union coming up. Animosity toward the union was visible as management reacted to each new union move.

An organization development specialist, who was auditing the development effort, was present at one such typical meeting. Following a review of the usual complaint, this specialist suggested,

"Why not experiment with the situation toward searching out a solution for it? Rather than continually complaining, why not try to solve the basic problems? Why not find ways to get to the root of the problem, rather than engaging, as you have done, in actions which appear to have the purpose of antagonizing the union?"

These questions caught management by surprise. Up to this point, their thinking and planning had been from a win-lose orientation. It was sufficient to bring such thinking to an abrupt halt. The intervention served as the basis for considering the impact of such a Union-Management Laboratory, and how it might be brought about.

Finally agreeing that such an effort could do no harm, though with low expectations that it would be of any substantial help, management concluded that it would be worth a try. They were ready to seek conditions where the mental attitude would be, "agreement is possible."

Agreement reached—with reservations. The assistant general manager arranged a conference between himself and the International business representative to propose the laboratory. The union officers eventually agreed to such a laboratory, but actually felt that "management's intention was to get them, one way or another." Thus, the question was, "How could such a meeting be of any real merit?"

The union was also reluctant because it felt that somewhere there was an invisible gimmick. They suspected a management strategy that would put the union in an even more difficult position. Other reservations included the possibility that the methods would result in some kind of brain washing and "softening up" of the union. Nonetheless, it was agreed to schedule the arrangement.

Union Representatives

Those attending the Union-Management Laboratory to represent the union included the International's business agent, the local president, the vice-president and others in the union hierarchy. In all, nine union members participated.

Management Representatives

An equal number of plant management personnel participated. The nine included the assistant general manager, the head of administrative services, the employee relations manager, and his field representative, a general foreman, two unit supervisors, and two first-line supervisors.

Participation of Behavorial Scientists

Two behavorial scientists conducted the Laboratory. One met with the management group; the other with the union. Both attended the joint sessions. The behavioral scientists familiarized themselves with the intergroup conflict that existed between the groups. Beyond that, neither of the professional participants acted under any prior agreement, with either group, to conduct himself in a specific manner. There was no prior agreement in any way to orient the issues discussed or to "guide" the discussion.

These, then, were the conditions and background considerations for the following description. The International union and management came together, tentatively, under conditions of great mutual suspicion, to test one another. There was little real belief in either party's mind that the Laboratory would be of any constructive help. On the other hand, there was genuine, unstated conviction that they might be able to force the other into capitulation, rather than creating a bond of soundness in the relationship.

DESCRIPTION OF THE EVENTS DURING THE UNION-MANAGEMENT INTERGROUP LABORATORY

Steps in Conducting the Union-Management Laboratory

The general arrangements of the Union-Management Laboratory are summarized in Table 1. Shown are the content or activity involved in each of the eight steps, and the time allocated. These were discussed more fully previously. Table 1, then, is a literal description of how this Union-Management Laboratory was conducted.

TABLE 1. Sequence of and Time Devoted to the Phases of the
Union-Management Intergroup Laboratory.

Phase	Activity	Time (Hours)
1	Orientation	½
2	Intragroup development of own image and its image of the other	5
3	Exchange of images across groups	1
4	Clarification of images	2
5	Intragroup diagnosis of present relationship	4
6	Exchange of diagnoses across groups	3
7	Consolidation of key issues and sources of friction	2
8	Planning next steps	1

Orientation of Participants to the Laboratory

At the outset, management and union got together for a brief orientation. The behavioral scientists in charge pictured the purpose, ground rules and background considerations involved.

The senior behavioral scientist began by saying "During these next two days, we wish to explore the problems that are blocking your relationship—to identify them and, if possible, to plan constructive steps for their elimination.

"Therefore, we are not concerned with issues of bargaining, problems of grievance handling, or attitudes about problems now being arbitrated. Nor, are we concerned with personalities. Rather, the key concern will be with the *character* of the relationship between your two groups and with the strategies which have characterized the two of you in the past."

It was further emphasized that this intergroup laboratory might be regarded as a first activity in a sequence of events, rather than as an interaction which would bring about a resolution of the differences or of concrete problems that needed to be solved.

The First Activity—Intergroup Development of Images

Following this orientation, the groups received their initial two-part assignment. First, each group, meeting separately, was asked to write a description—an image—of how it saw itself, particularly in its relationship with the other group. Secondly, each group was asked to develop an image of how it saw the other group's behavior. These images were to be written on large newsprint for use when the two groups reconvened.

The Union's reaction to the task. Union members had great difficulty understanding the task. A false start took them into a discussion of issues surrounding a recently completed bargaining session. The session began with strong leadership from the business agent with support from the union secretary.

After several minutes, the behavioral scientist intervened. He redefined the task for them. "The present task is to describe the *character*, the quality, of the relationship; that is, typical behavior and attitudes. The task is *not* to debate technical and legalistic issues."

At the beginning, then, the union members did not have the concept of examining the *process* of behavior—to examine and discuss actions, feelings and attitudes. Their thinking pattern was so deeply ingrained on the *content* side that they were not able to think about the dynamics of the relationship except as they happened to erupt in content terms. It must be said, then, that to step back from content and to take a process approach proved to be very, very, tough for the union. Eventually, however, they were able to do so.

After the intervention by the behavorial scientist, the secretary, addressing the business agent, said, "I think we should caucus before we go any further!"

This proposal was interrupted by the behavorial scientist, who stated, "Look, if this cannot be discussed in my presence, then there is little hope that anything will be achieved in the next two days."

This intervention was followed by several moments of silence. Several union members exchanged glances, but no one spoke. Finally, the business agent began again. Gradually, tediously, the discussion shifted toward a detailed picturing of the union's behavior and attitudes of their relationship with management. Participation gradually spread among all members.

Management's Approach to the Initial Task. Management launched into this first task with a feeling of confidence. They were sure they could quickly put their finger on the real problems. In line with management's feeling toward the business agent, they predicted, "He (the business agent) will call all the shots—he and his two stooges, Smith (the secretary), and Jones (the president). No one else will speak up. The rest will just sit back and go along."

In contrast to the union, *management had the process orientation.* This is not to say that process examination came easy for them, but they did have the concept. They quickly developed a strategy of work and moved into the task.

Management decided to develop its own image first, but ran into trouble. Their relationship with the union was so antagonistic that discussion of their own image repeatedly slipped into a discussion of the union. They spoke of union personalities. They accused the clique in the next meeting room of being the source of all frictions. One management member said, "Basically, the union members are good solid citizens. It's a shame five or six power-mad guys are running things."

A first-line supervisor said, "I've got some of the best, hard-working guys in the plant that are members of this union. We really work together. But, I can't even talk with these union officials. I just 'see red' and clam up every time I see one of them coming. Jones, (the president) began stirring up trouble the day he joined the union. That was fifteen years ago. I was president of the union myself at the time."

At this point, the behavioral scientist intervened. "As I understand it, you plan to develop your own image first, and then to develop that of the union. Obviously, you are having difficulty doing this. Your own image is repeatedly forgotten and union behavior and personalities keep coming into the picture. Everyone wants to get something off his chest. Let me suggest that you might table your own image for the time being and begin on that of the union. If this moves easier, then stay with it. Having done this, you may find it easier to talk about your own behavior. Alternatively, you might work on both images simultaneously as thoughts about either occur to you, or when parallel behavior is seen in both groups."

This intervention caused management to pause and examine how it was working. Black, the employee relations manager, spoke up, "Let's admit it. They are no damn angels, but neither are we. Let's get a mirror up here where we can see ourselves, and put down what we see, whether we like it or not."

Someone volunteered to record. The assistant plant manager summarized key points he thought should be in their own image. Management decided to continue with its own image. This time they stuck with it.

The Next Step: Management and the International Exchange Images

As might be predicted, it was easier for both management and the union to discover and discuss negative aspects of the other's attitudes and behavior than of their own. On the other hand, the goodness of one's own intentions and the rightness of one's attitudes came quite easily. Despite such unevenness, there were areas of agreement in the images and counter-images developed by the two. However, misinterpretations and misunderstandings were frequent and deep.

Management's Image of Itself

The exchange of images took place in the general session room. The union, not wanting to start first, waited for management to volunteer. This management did readily. They were eager to set the union straight on a few matters.

In its self-image, management concentrated on its present actions and intentions regarding the union, although past events were considered to draw distinctions and to point up changes. The following quotations are from the report management gave to the union representatives during the intergroup exchange in Phase III.

Running the business. The outstanding feature of management's image of itself was its concern for plant business—its structural organization, operations and economic health. About these matters, management was sure and clear.

"Today we are more competitive and aggressive than ever. There is a drive among us to make the plant grow—to maintain and increase our competitive edge. There is a sense of urgency in the way we meet our problems. We are no longer content merely to maintain our present economic position. We are trying continually to do a better job. Just in the past two years, we feel a need to *change*—to change the way we do things; to create and innovate, and to try out new things. It is fantastic when you think of the many directions we now know to move once we began to think this way."

Feelings of increased autonomy and responsibility. "Several years ago, headquarters began to recognize a strong trend to greater decentralization. Because of decentralization and our own boot-straps efforts, we now have a greater feeling of responsibility for all economic decisions. Now, nothing slips by without being closely examined and questioned. We examine our decisions from a longer-term perspective."

One manager put it this way, "We view ourselves as the stewards of a large financial, physical, and social responsibility. Yet, despite increased headquarters, economic and competitive pressures, *we have greater confidence.* More than even two years ago, we have a greater sense of security in our position; we are more confident of *our ability to manage.*"

Quality of supervision. Another major point in management's self-image was its concern for supervision at all levels.

"One of our most critical responsibilities is to upgrade supervision. We have come a long way in this direction, but we still have a long way to go. More than ever, we feel the constant need for tighter supervision. We expect leaner operations, and we are getting it. Idle or unproductive time must be eliminated wherever it exists."

Another added, "Sure, we still feel some pressure from headquarters. But, in addition, we are putting pressure on ourselves. This isn't something just being pushed down the line. At every level there is a constant push for leaner operations. I don't think this is temporary. The *character* of our effort is shifting away from the good old days. We are not waiting for a dip in the economy to wake us up. We are just getting started. It is a kind of dynamic movement—an upswing—not the kind of spurts we used to get into when the economy got a little tough.

"Management is more hard-nosed today, yet people are fiercely loyal. The whole community is with us 100 per cent."

Relations with the international. The third major aspect of management's self-image concerned its relations with the International union. As will be seen later, it is here that the greatest distortion existed between how management viewed itself and how the union interpreted management's intentions and actions.

Despite past events, management expressed a concern to solve problems between itself and the International. Historically, headquarters and local management had demonstrated a preference for dealing with independent unions. In this connection, management expressed a current desire ". . . to treat the International just as we do independents. We need to learn to live with them. Our goal is to establish a sound problem-solving relationship with the International. But it won't be easy. Up to now, you have fought our step in this direction. This doesn't mean we are trying to go soft. Nor does it mean we are tossing in the towel. We just want to get to the bottom of this running battle."

The division manager added, "What really 'bugs' you is that this situation is out of character with our other efforts. Sure, we feel a certain resentment toward the International—all unions for that matter—because of the many restrictions they impose on us. We feel that they are a limiting—a restraining force. Part of this is because we feel that greater power will go to the government, or up into headquarters if we don't manage effectively. To do this, we need freedom to act. We feel the obligation to maintain our right to manage—to run things in the best interest of the business."

Management acknowledged that it had demonstrated little concern to *work with* this International in the past. On this point, they remarked, "We have been inconsistent over the years in our relations with the International. Because of our preference for independents, we have treated you one way and the independents another. We have always pushed and fought International harder than the independents. Now, when you see us coming and you start swinging. I guess, in the past, we felt this was the way headquarters expected us to treat you and other internationals, although there never has been a written policy to this effect."

Seeking power. Although they were not able to put the issue into clear perspective, another major concern of management was that the International might gain even greater power. Local union management was seen to be working for more power—more "wins" to prove itself. If this were to happen, management felt that other internationals might again gain a foothold in the plant. This fear was expressed in a number of ways.

"For this reason, we negotiate contracts to give management maximum flexibility. It is important that we continue to do so if we are to run the business in a sound manner. In those areas that are not clear in the contract, the interest of the company must be foremost.

"In the old days, we practically gave things away to the union. We can no longer afford to do this. Thus we are more legalistic in interpreting the contract. The way you pick at everything, we have to be legalistic. Yet, despite this and our preference for independents, we have always been honest and above board with the International. The contract is a set of obligations for both sides, and we live up to ours."

"We are more realistic now than we used to be," said another. "It is important that we not lose more power or rights to this union, or any other. We have to be concerned with the long-range, gradual loss of our power that could result if we yield on this point, give in here, go along on others, and so on. The International, on the other hand, is just concerned with today and with what is coming up that year. You are not worried about whether we will still be in business ten years from now."

Can the union measure up? Management had considerable doubt about the union's problem-solving and decision-making abilities. Also, management did not trust the union's intentions. "Beyond doing the work, just how much help operating could they give us?" was the question.

"Unions don't see things in the same perspective as we do. We have to look at the long haul. This means consideration of many facets of business that you are not even aware of, and this becomes more true as you move down the ranks.

"You want co-management. You want a say in every decision. We know what would happen if the union got such a position. You would be telling us how to run the business from top to bottom. You would start grabbing for more power, and we wouldn't be able to make a move without your blocking us. As we see it, we can't afford this. Although we want to involve people at all levels, the business is still our responsibility."

It is interesting to note that even during the period of exchange, as in its separate meeting, management found itself talking about the union in its own self-description more than was necessary to make comparisons.

Equal concern for people and production. Despite these disagreements, there were many areas in which management felt that cooperative problem-solving was possible. In such areas, management wanted greater union involvement before reaching decisions.

"The fact that we are here today shows we want to work out our problems with the International—that we are willing to reach joint decisions. Years ago, production perhaps was our only concern. There then came a time when the company practically gave in on everything that concerned people. Now, we want to move, and are moving, toward a more equal concern for production and people. Our present organization improvement effort demonstrates we are trying to move in that direction. We communicate more freely now, and through the unions 'cut in' the people on what's going on."

Management completed the image of itself at this point. The behavioral scientist asked if either group had any questions of clarification. During management's presentation, the union had said nothing. At the outset, the behavioral scientist had cautioned both groups against asking questions to belittle, to "explain" or to rationalize what was being said. Participants were told that such actions would make it difficult for them to "hear" what was actually being said. At the same time, questions aimed at defending one's group would make it difficult for people to express themselves openly and candidly. Thus, not knowing how to speak except in defense, union members made no comments. They would wait for their opportunity to have the floor.

There being no questions, management moved into describing its image of the union. However, for comparison purposes, and while management's image of itself is still fresh, let's jump forward in time to hear the union describe how it saw management.

The International's Image of Management

The local business agent spoke for the union. In contrast with management's self-image, the union's image was short, crisp, and to the point. And, even then, the major points of the union have been collapsed into one simple statement: "This company is opposed to organized labor in any form, shape or manner!"

Down with organized labor. "Management has pulled every trick in the book to get us and other internationals out of the plant. The only reason you prefer independents is because you think they are the lesser of two evils. At best, you want a home grown union.

"There is not a man in this plant, or anyone within 200 miles, who doesn't know that this company is against unions. This has been headquarters' policy for 30 years. And, you guys follow it right down the line. Don't tell us about 'increased responsibility.' Why don't you tell the real facts. Headquarters is putting the pressure on you. 'Cut costs'—that's what they are saying. And that means, 'get the International out.' Then you could trim people and jobs as you see fit because no one would be here to stand up to you. Your independents don't. You see to that."

At this, the division manager could no longer contain himself. "Do you mean that you really believe there is some formal policy in headquarters that says, sometime in the future, we are to be rid of all international unions?"

The business agent continued as if he had not been interrupted. "The company, and that means *this plant*—we make no distinction —has long-range plans *to abolish all international unions in every plant*. We are your target here. So don't talk to us about equal concern for people. Even if you wanted them, good relations are impossible. It boils down to one simple thing. Local management is dictated to by company policy. They say 'jump' and you say, 'how high?' Your hands are tied and you know it."

Handling grievances. The second point in the union's image of management was the way in which management handled grievances. "You deal with us in bad faith. The ink isn't dry on a document, and you are already violating its terms. It makes us sick how you give us the run-around on grievances. Every supervisor tells a different story and gets away with it. A supervisor's word is always taken against us. And the supervisors lie. They tell a different story every time they talk about an incident. They make the 'facts' fit.

"We weren't born yesterday, Mr. Brown," the business agent directed his remark to the assistant plant manager. "Management tries to make the International appear ineffective to the workers by failing to settle grievances. And what a farce that is! You have a predetermined answer to every kind of grievance. All you do is reach into your file of pat answers from headquarters and try to shove them down our throats."

Brown, the assistant plant manager, interrupted to ask, "I wish you would give us a specific example. I sometimes wish there were pat answers. It would sure make it easier for me. I just spent a whole weekend and three nights reviewing a case, trying to make a proper judgment. Personally, I thought I did a good job. You know which one I mean."

"Mr. Brown," the business agent returned, "I don't know what you were looking for in that case. I'm sure it *wasn't* loopholes, but if you were looking for the facts, they were right there in black and white. We gave them to you when the grievance first came up."

The assistant plant manager started to reply. Shaking his head, however, he said nothing. The business agent continued. "Management has yet to base a decision on the merits of a case because it fits right into your scheme to get rid of us. You try to force arbitration on *every* grievance. You know we don't have the money to take every single case to arbitration. You want to break us. Management makes us get a different arbitrator for every single case. You refuse to let an arbitrator try two or three cases at the same time, so that it wouldn't cost as much."

This time the employee relations manager stepped in. "Boy, I swear. Sometimes you sound like a broken record. How many times have we discussed this? You know why we don't like an arbitrator to try two cases at the same time. If an arbitrator renders a decision in favor of one party, then he is very likely to render the next one in favor of the other. Many arbitrators have a tendency to even things out. We don't like it because we don't feel each case gets a good sound decision, based solely on merit. We are not going to get a bad decision or establish a precedent just because some arbitrator's conscience gets the best of him."

"We are well aware of what you say, Mr. Black," the union secretary said. "But, you have yet to show us any evidence that such things really happen. Do you believe all arbitrators are crooked?"

"I didn't say that," Black returned. "I said there is a *tendency* for this to happen. I don't know of any arbitrator who would consciously do such a thing. And, I would like to correct what you said in the beginning. There is evidence that decisions are split more when they are tried in pairs. You have seen it."

Management is a 'fatherly dictator.' The union's major point referred to what the union saw in management as paternalism. "Most management people think they are three stories taller than the workers. Management is a fatherly dictator. We all have one father—we don't need another one. We are not permitted to make one single decision for ourselves. We can't even decide what kind of benefits we want. You tell us how much we should save, what type of insurance we should take out, how much to donate to charity, when to take vacations, when to retire, etc., etc., etc. The worst part is that you try to tell us how to practice the skill it has taken most of us twenty years or more to learn and develop."

Controlling the apprenticeship program. "You try to tell us what our apprenticeship policies should be. You did away with the training committee we used to jointly administer, but, who should know better than *us* the skills and training a craftsman should have? And look how management has flopped. Last year, you unilaterally entered six people into *your* training program. How many passed? None! The only way a guy can get decent training is to work alongside one of us until he learns the ropes."

Loss in union membership. The International placed the problems of dwindling membership squarely in management's lap.

"Management has been chipping away at our membership for five years. More work is contracted. You get outside personnel to do our work and pay them a dollar and a half less. You have already run out one international. We are the only sizeable one left, and you are trying to gradually starve us out.

"There was a time when we could take pride in our work. We were consulted on how to do jobs and various projects. Now you just *tell* us. There is nothing to a job but the money in it."

Production is number one. "Production and profits are number one on your list. They have to be—that is your job, and headquarters won't let you forget it. That's why we have to take steps to keep you from running over our people. You're interested in a man only for what you can get out of him."

The two faces of management. "In spite of everything headquarters and plant managers have said and done, they deny publicly that they are against unions. When the last International got voted out, you were going around telling everyone how much you liked the International. You went through the motions of negotiating a new contract with them. But all the time you were doing everything you could to get them out. All we can say is, 'Don't start loving us, or we really *will* begin to worry'!"

"It boils down to this," the business agent concluded. "We don't have this people-production concern you claim to have, which, anyway you look at it, has 'dollar signs' written all over it. Our job is people. In this respect, we are out to do the best job we can. And, we'll push as hard as we have to if that is what it takes."

The Combined Images of Management

Before going into the description of the union's self-image and how it, in turn, is viewed by management, let us briefly review the two images of management. At this point, both sides can only see differences. The more important question, though, is, "Are there similarities which, although not seen by either side, could become the foundation of common effort?"

Table 2 summarizes some of the key issues and characteristics in management's self-image and in the union's image of management. It also shows union's image of itself and management's counter-image of the union which will be described in the following sections.

In short, management says it wants to run the business in the best manner it knows how. It *is* concerned with production and profits, *but* at the same time, it has an interest in people. Management says it shows greater concern for people now. It wants to involve people at all levels in running the operations effectively. This includes working in a problem-solving manner with the International. However, management insists on its "right to manage." It recognizes its obligations to the union, and it lives up to them.

Now, what does the union see? What did it "hear" during the exchange? "Management is out to break the International. Management is scheming and underhanded. It deals in bad faith. Management is a pawn to headquarters."

Already, deep differences have arisen. But, embedded in these differences are similarities neither party sees, particularly the union with respect to management's image. These differences and similarities will become sharper as we move through the images of the union. At this point though, the union does not see or hear management's interest in people. Yet, like the union, management says it is concerned with people. All of the union's interpretation of management is given to management's *production* concerns. And the union sees much of this being "pushed" down from company Headquarters. The International and management agree on management's past preference for independents. But, the International sees this as meaning that management is openly against internationals. "Either you are 'for' something, or else you are 'against' it," was the union's attitude.

TABLE 2. "Self" and "Other" Images Developed by Management
and the International Union During Phase II of the
Union-Management Laboratory.

Management's Image

Of Itself	By The Union
1. Concerned with running the business effectively	1. . . . . (an issue not considered)
2. We show equal concern for production and people	2. Management is concerned only with production
3. Autonomous decentralized decision-making body	3. They follow all of headquarters' policies and dictates
4. Want to learn to work better with international	4. Opposed to all organized labor
5. Prefer to deal with independent unions	5. Prefer to deal with independent unions
6. Strive continually to upgrade supervision	6. . . . .
7. Goal is to establish problem-solving relationship with the international	7. Their goal is to drive us out of the plant
8. Maintain flexibility in areas concerning our "rights to manage"	8. Management wants power and control over every aspect of a worker's life—they are "fatherly dictators"
9. We are inconsistent in how we treat independents and the international	9. They treat the independents one way and us another
10. Honest and above-board in our dealings	10. They are underhanded and they lie

The Union's Image

By Management	Of Itself
1. Little concern shown for the profit picture of the company	1. Concerned primarily with **people**
2. They are skillful and have intense pride	2. Proud of our craft and skills
3. Controlled by a scheming professional leader and a minority clique	3. We are governed by the will of the total membership
4. Legalistic and rigid in interpreting contract	4. Approach problems and contract with open mind
5. The union pushes every grievance to the point of arbitration. When they want to establish a precedent, they want to arbitrate	5. Do not want to have to arbitrate every grievance. We want to work them out with management
6. They want to prove they can "win"—they don't care what, just so it is something	6. We want good relations and to solve our problems with management
7. They want to co-manage. They want a say in every decision we make	7. We want a voice in those areas that directly concern us
8. The union wants the training of their people back under their control	8. We want joint control of the training and apprenticeship program
9. The union does not communicate internally. Their people don't know what is going on	9. Our people always know what is going on and what important union business is coming up
10. Union is concerned only with seniority and job security. They are not concerned with our problems	10. We want greater consideration for our skills and what we can contribute to the plant

The Self-Image of the International Union

How management in turn saw the union is cast against this self-image in the next section. Again, the union was brief. The business agent reported for the International.

People-oriented. "We have different goals," the union said. "Management's only concern is production and profit. We, on the other hand, are interested in *people*. Our job is to see that our workers get everything that is coming to them, although this is not to say we don't care how the work is done. We are craftsmen. We do a job as skillfully as possible. We return a fair day's work for a fair day's pay. We recognize our responsibility to the company and to the community."

Seeking sound relations. The union reported it was tired of the constant battle with management.

"The union is eager to establish good relations, which is why we are here today. However, our attitudes are affected by our relationship with the company. Maybe our attitude is not what it should be, but it depends on management's action. If you start to lean on us, we'll push back.

"We think we approach problems with an open mind. We believe our problems can be settled, but, we are not dropping our 'guard' until we are sure what management will do."

Democratic-autonomous international. "Union policies are dictated by local members. Unlike plant management, we don't have to follow the party line of our headquarters. We don't make a decision before going to the members to see what they want.

"All this union has ever sought is steady work; a chance to do a good job and job security for its members. We expect management to respond to our honesty and integrity in the same manner—to treat us like adults, not children."

At this point, the division manager asked "How can you say you represent the total membership when only about 10 per cent turn out for the meetings? I know you guys have to be there so that's about the whole 10 per cent right there."

"I don't know out of what hat you pulled your figures," the

union secretary returned, "but our regular attendance is well above that. At the last wage discussion, over 75 per cent was there. Sure, fewer attend when there is nothing at stake. We like to watch television, too."

"As far as day-to-day business is concerned," the business agent added, "We are like any organization. A small group of administrators always 'runs the business,' as you say. Does everyone always attend all of your meetings? Of course not."

We communicate. "The important thing is," the business agent continued, "our people know what is going on. We keep them informed on the issues. Somebody has to. They would never know a thing if we didn't. When an important local issue is coming up, we let them know well in advance."

Problem-solving approach. "We try to work out our problems, grievances for example, with you. We try to settle them as they come up. But, you guys block us every way we turn. We can't work any other way with you, push, push, push. But, at least we deal in good faith. Our cards are always on the table."

Apprenticeship program. "We feel there should again be a joint training committee. It is important to us, and it should be to the company, to maintain high standards. But, you can't get high standards when we have no control over the training our people get."

Just recognition. "Management has never given us the recognition our skills and craftsmanship merit. To you, it's just another job. You wouldn't recognize a good piece of work if it was staring you in the face. We contribute a lot to plant operations. And, much more could be contributed with half a chance. The International should have a voice in whatever affects our work and livelihood. We don't want co-management. We want the recognition we deserve, and a chance to contribute. The union is damn proud of its skills, and the work it can do."

The business agent concluded at this point. "That's it," he said.

Management raised several questions regarding "just how well" the union actually communicated with its membership. Both sides became argumentative. One behavorial scientist suggested they move on to the next image. He said, "Right now both of you are banging at each other, and I'm sure this could go on for some time. But I don't think any real understanding will come from this. So unless someone wants to ask a question to insure he heard something correctly, I suggest we move ahead."

There were no questions.

To complete the final image, the total relationship, management's counter-image of the union, was described.

Management's Image of the Union

The counter-image of the union, as seen by management, presents a different picture than that of the union's self-image.

Centralized control. "We see the union as controlled by a small minority which doesn't represent the full thinking of its membership. The leadership comes from a professional union man. He has a personal motive for everything he does. He is trying to build his reputation to get a higher job in the International. This local is just a stepping stone for him. He gets his instructions from International headquarters. The International has a platform it wants to get into every local.

"Along with the business agent, as we see it, three or four rabble rousers keep the membership stirred up. They all work in the X part of the plant where the best jobs are. That is all they care about. No one else goes to meetings. The people in the field don't have a voice or stake in most decisions.

"The union leaders don't trust management, and they don't want to. They want to co-manage the business. They want to have a say in every decision."

Restricted communications. "Most of the members don't know what is going on. They have a feeling of insecurity because their leadership doesn't communicate with them. That is how they are controlled. The leadership sees to it that they don't trust management. You keep fanning the fires."

Hard bargainers. Management reported that the International acted like a real tough union. "You fight us every step of the way.

All you really care about is winning. You don't care what is won, just so it's something. Union leaders want to demonstrate to the membership that they are successful. You use more force and pressure on us in bargaining than any of the other unions. Every point in the contract is given a rigid, legalistic interpretation. Everything is black or white. The union won't yield or compromise on a thing."

Union rules are against sound business. "Rates and seniority are all that count in the union. It is impossible for us to get the best man into a job because of seniority rules. This isn't good business. And, it is no good for the people who have the skills, but can't move up."

Proud and skilled craftsmen. "The people in the union have pride in their skills; in their work. Yet, they are content to be run by a small clique—up to going over the deep end—*a strike*. You found out the last time you tried to get your people to take a strike vote. Things would be different if the people had more say in union affairs."

The Union's Composite Image

In the union leaders' eyes, then, they are the democratic agents of the International local's membership. All important decisions are made by the total membership. Union leaders communicate with the membership. The union is a proud and skillful group, but feels management doesn't recognize this. The union wants a voice in those matters that involve them, *e.g.,* the apprenticeship training program. The union wants and has tried to work out their problems with management, without going outside, *e.g.,* arbitration, but the union feels management doesn't want to work with it. The union leaders feel obligated to represent and stand up for their membership. Their job, as they see it, is "people."

Management recognizes the union is a proud and skillful group, but the union doesn't sense this. The union wants to be involved more in the operations of the plant and management expressed the same desire, but neither sees this as a common interest at this point.

In contrast to the union's self-image, management feels the union is run by a clique that is controlled by International headquarters. Management feels the union membership is unaware of this—"They are good, solid citizens, but they don't know the score because union leaders don't communicate with them." Management feels the union has a typical union interest in people only, *i.e.*, seniority, rates, etc. In short, management feels the problems are lodged in union leadership.

As can be seen, despite common interest, a wide gulf separated union and management views at the outset of the laboratory. At this point, there was perhaps even less confidence on both sides than initially, that the two would be able to achieve any understanding or resolution of differences. There, then, were the "raw materials" participants had to work with during the night and day remaining in the laboratory.

These misunderstandings and differences are not uncommon, however, for groups with a long history of conflict.

Do Images Lie? A Need for Clarification

The next two hours were spent in a joint session over the images each had presented. Neither side could believe the other could be so "wrong." At times the discussion, designed to clarify, became heated and sharp. Each side quickly forgot its good intentions to work in a problem-solving manner. Without interventions by the behavioral scientists to focus what was taking place, it is likely the discussion would have slipped into typical win-lose exchange of vindictive accusations.

"Little will be gained," one of the behavioral scientists said by way of intervention, "at the present rate. All I can hear is one side explaining to the other, why it is right and the other is wrong. *The purpose of this session is to clarify what has emerged in your images.* This is to insure that both of you clearly understand the behavior, attitudes, feelings and intentions of the other. If common understanding is not achieved at this level, then it is likely both of you will continue to misinterpret each other's intentions and actions. Rather than discovering a common basis on which to build, differences and resulting antagonism will keep you apart."

However, the need to "bang" one another was too strong. For example, the International continued to hammer at its point that management intended to slowly drive them from the plant. Management in turn answered with denials and countercharges.

Eventually, one of the behavorial scientists again intervened. "It still appears that little is being heard because people are so pre-occupied with defending what they say and denying what others are saying. Here is a suggestion. Make sure you understand what each has said up to this point. Disregard whether you agree or not. If one of you says 'the moon is made of blue cheese,' then the other wants to be clear that he said 'blue cheese' and not Swiss, or something else. Whether you agree with this description of the moon is not what we want to accomplish at this time."

Several guarded questions followed this intervention, and it was obvious most were suppressing the urge to move back to the attack. Not wanting openly to resume their previous line of questioning yet not knowing how and not trusting themselves to seek further clarification, members from both groups waited for the other to make the next move.

The behavorial scientist again intervened with the following suggestion. "If no further clarification is needed, then for the remainder of the evening and for, let's say the first two hours in the morning, more might be accomplished if both groups devote themselves to answering fully the following questions: One, what is it we do (the union or management) that has contributed to the image the other group has of us? Secondly, what is it in *our own beliefs and actions* that leads us to the conclusion we have reached about ourselves? To do this, take with you the images on newsprint that the other group developed. In this way, you can focus on the issues and characteristics described by the other group."

Phase V—A Need for Self-Insight and Understanding

Phase V, self-diagnosis, is a pivotal point in the Union-Management Laboratory. The need at this point is for both sides to look underneath surface tensions to discover *why* the relationship has become what it is.

Diagnosing self- and counter-images. Both groups, meeting separately, spent the evening and part of the following morning, in self-analysis and diagnosing the why of their own actions. Gradually, as the *reactions* and feelings of the other groups were tested against the actions under examination, their behavior no longer appeared so inappropriate. Although still far from any real degree of mutual trust or understanding, the door at least was open for both management and the union, to see what actions would need to be understood and shifted to achieve a sound problem-solving relationship.

Management's approach to the diagnosis. Upon returning to their meeting room, management began by berating the union's "gross misunderstandings."

One manager remarked, "I told you! Anything he (the business agent) said, the others would back up. Those guys don't even know what is fact and what is fiction."

Another said, "If they want to believe that stuff and keep fighting us, I would just as soon let them run. They are not big enough or strong enough to bother us. Let them strike later if they want. I doubt if they would. But, if they did, we could run the business fine without them . . . better!"

"How could they be so wrong?" others chimed in.

"I think they really know," the first came back. "It fits everything they do. They always use this tactic. We're always the 'scheming' ones and *they* are the 'innocent' ones. The business agent has been to the International's school. They taught him all the tricks."

This self-justification continued for several mintues before the behavioral scientist intervened. "What you are doing now is not likely to move you toward better understanding with the union. First, you are disregarding your initial commitment to work during the laboratory in a problem-solving manner. This will defeat why you are here and any progress made up to this point. Secondly, working through the present task, as it is intended, can help both you and the union to move toward the 'nub' of what has brought about these wide differences."

At this, the employee relations manager made the following proposal, "Let's take their image of us as it is on the newsprint, and just start listing everything we can think of under each one of their points that could possibly lie behind how they interpret us."

The proposal was picked up and management went to work.

The union's reaction. Meanwhile, the union reacted in a similar fashion. Management, as far as they were concerned, had demonstrated that the union had been right all along.

"How can they honestly think that we are a clique running our organization?" the president asked.

"The whole problem," the business agent answered, "is that they are still living in the 19th century. They can't understand that unions are here to stay. They have no concept of the ideology of unions."

The union rationalized on the issue that the leadership, all except two members, did, in fact, work in that part of the plant containing the better jobs. Other content issues also were raised. But gradually union members began to get a feel for process examination. They moved rapidly into digging into their attitudes and feelings, and into their reactions to the images developed by management.

Both groups worked on this task until past 10:00 p.m. They picked up again at 8:00 the next morning, and completed their tasks around 10:00 a.m.

Phase VI: Meshing Insights on an Interchange Basis

Following the individual diagnosis of their own behavior and their "contributions" to the relationship, management and the union came back together. Most of the day was devoted to exchanging and then debating through the results of both groups' diagnoses.

Management's Diagnosis of the Union's Image of Management

In its diagnosis, management took the five main characteristics of itself as the union had listed them.

The five major points were as follows:

1. The company is opposed to all International (affiliated) unions.

2. Management denies publicly that it is opposed to unions to maintain good public image.

3. The company has long-range plans to abolish international unions.

4. The company is a fatherly dictator.

5. Local (plant) management is dictated to by headquarters' policy, which makes good relations impossible.

Under each item, management had listed contributions (past events and actions) that they felt (they and the company) had contributed to this image. This list was quite full; so full in fact, that management did not get to diagnosing the union's image of itself, except as it happened to relate to the management's image. The union, on the other hand, was more brief, but had studied both its own and management's images.

The assistant plant manager, as he had done earlier during Phase III, began the interchange. The first item he discussed was the number 1 issue so far as the union was concerned; namely "The company is opposed to International (affiliated) unions." Management cited a number of instances where it could have left such an impression in the union's mind. However, it was pointed out that management did not view the statement as an accurate description of its present thinking.

Why management looks anti-union. "We looked around," the assistant plant manager said, "in the whole organization, as well as in the plant, to see what past actions could lead you to think we are against affiliated unions. I'd like to cite a few. But, before I do, let me clearly say again that we *prefer* independent unions, but this does not mean that we are opposed to internationals.

"What are some of the examples? For one, Mr.————————, the now retired company president, made a public statement several years ago to the effect that we preferred company unions, and that the company would try to keep internationals out. Of course, as you know, in 1959, the X International was voted in. At that time, Mr.————————, the plant manager, in a letter to all employees, stated he was sorry to see this and that management hoped that the independent would get back in. However, he did not say that we would not cooperate with the X International, as long as it was in.

"More generally, the whole company can be characterized as being relatively void of affiliated unions. You can count them on the fingers of your right hand, if you look at all plants. On top of this, our plant is sitting right in a sea of the *X* International. It is represented in at least seven plants I can think of, within a 50-mile radius."

Impact of economy moves. "Closer to home, many of our own and the company's economy moves have not been seen as such. Rather, they have been interpreted as efforts to get rid of the internationals, particularly the *X* International, until it was voted out last summer. Our recent layoff falls in this category. The closing of a nearby plant by the company is another. Most employees have the impression that headquarters would not make investments or expansions of our plant as long as the International was in."

The International's business agent interrupted to ask, "And isn't this true? The company hasn't made any investments in the plant in over four years. It has at others. We think this is a big reason why you go right along with the policy, 'no affiliated unions!' "

"But, you are still saying there is no difference between what headquarters thinks and what *we* here at the plant think," the assistant plant manager returned.

"We make no distinction whatsoever," the business agent replied. "You can't afford to do anything else. Why don't you go to our second point. That's where the facts are. To maintain your public image, you deny opposition to affiliated unions, but that doesn't square with the facts. You said, yourself, the company prefers independents."

"But this is still not to say we are opposed to internationals. We only say we prefer independents," the employee relations manager interrupted. "You are here now, have been for over 25 years, and we expect you to be here for a long time to come. We want to work with you, but it is awfully hard when you think the opposite. In many ways, headquarters has tried to cover up its opposition to internationals. But, this is not as true at headquarters today. And it certainly isn't true at this plant.

"Maybe a couple of points we came up with under your second point—that we deny publicly our opposition—can clarify what we are saying here."

Failure to take a stand. "We think you get this impression through our *omission* to support or reject International, particularly in the recent case of the *X* International. You recall, we took no stand during the certification election. We *publicly* said we were not going to support the Independent or the International. Our silence may give you the impression that we *deny* our opposition to unions."

"Do you deny that you were pleased when the Independent won out?" the union president asked.

"No. I can't help but say that we were honestly pleased. But, had the International won, we would have continued to bargain in good faith and to fulfill our obligations. Right up to the election, we were still negotiating with them."

Bargaining in bad faith. "You were just going through the motions to maintain your false image," the business agent said. "In the background you were doing all you could to make the International appear incompetent. This is what you are doing to us. And, you were getting your orders straight from headquarters. Look at the wage issue. Your offer is ridiculous, way below the straight rate, just to embarrass the International. We think local management would have offered a just amount had you been free to do so. But the whole problem is that you were not free. How can you say you deal with us in good faith and cooperate with us when you *cannot* because of headquarters?"

"Let me answer that," the assistant plant manager continued, "by covering your points 3 and 5 which tie in. But first, let me reply to what you said about the wage issue. At our *Y* plant, the *X* Union was offered the straight rate because it did not put plant *Y* out of line in its area. We offered less because to do otherwise would have put us way out of line with the rates in our area. We were among the top 5 at that time. Even then, we offered the *X* Union an increase that would have put us above everyone. All this is to say that headquarters' position on wages is that plants *should exercise local responsibility to keep rates in line.* Its policy is *not* to use wages to punish unions.

"Now, in 3, you say, 'the company has long-range plans to abolish international unions, especially ours.' In 5 you say, 'local management is dictated to by headquarter's policy.' We can't answer why you feel we are 'out to get you.' We don't know really how to answer your belief that we lack local autonomy, except by denial and to say in the most honest way we know, that we make our own decisions. And as far as this concerns this union, our decision is that we want to work with you in a sound manner."

"I wish we could believe that," the business agent said. Others nodded.

The assistant plant manager went on to cite other events the management group felt contributed to the union's belief that management had long-range designs to abolish affiliated unions. Included here was a recent reduction in rolls, the abolishment of two departments in which the employees were represented by international unions, contracting of work, and the movement of certain work performed by this union into areas represented by independents.

"That last one is a good example of why we say you do not act in good faith," the union secretary said. "Look at the change you made in the tool room. You said you were only making some physical changes, but before we knew it, the change resulted in different jobs. This was not what you led us to believe."

"We did not say there wouldn't be any changes in the jobs affected," a member of the management group returned. "You only assumed this."

Dealing above-board. "But it's always the same thing whether with grievances or what have you," the business agent countered. "You deal in half truths. If you really wanted to work with us, you wouldn't be so evasive. We think you should face the issues squarely and operate on the table with trust."

Legalism. "I'll give you another example," he continued, "and this probably is the biggest problem. Again, it's the way in which you deal with grievances. Rather than giving us a straightforward answer, you take a legalistic approach. Now this is what you accused us of earlier. But, I'm saying that if things are legalistic, it is because you have made them this way. This kind of legal approach stifles straightforward answers. But we feel this is only a minor part of the problem. You hide your real motives in the language of your written grievance decisions. And your interpretations to our grievances make us look childish to have even raised a grievance in the first place."

A Step Toward Understanding

Both groups now were openly exchanging their feelings and interpretations. For this reason, the behavioral scientists did not intervene when the discussion slid into the union picturing its analysis of management's counter-image. It was felt that, in this way, overlapping issues could be productively discussed as they were encountered. The interplay from this kind of interchange seemed to generate greater understanding for the moment than mechanically completing one group's presentation before moving to the next.

The Union's Summary of Its Diagnosis

"While we have been talking," the business agent said during a lull, "we have covered a number of the points we had to make with respect to your image of us. However, there are still some things we want to lay out on the table. So, unless there is more management has to add from the newsprints, I would like to summarize the remainder of our points."

Management responded that this would be good. They said, though, that they would like to be able to interrupt on some point if something the union said triggered a thought in their minds.

This approach was agreeable.

Independents are tools. "There is one point," the business agent began, "that is a basic, fundamental, ideological breach in the thinking of our two groups. We are not sure this can ever be patched— that is, your overriding preference for independent unions. I don't want to get into, *again,* whether this means management is 'opposed' to Internationals or not. But, I don't see how we can interpret so many arrows in this direction in any other way. In many companies, and especially this one, independent unions are set up to *deny* workers the freedom to bargain. When people do not have the freedom to select between an International *or* an Independent, then they do not have the proper freedom of choice. *And, people in this plant don't have that choice."*

The plant manager reacted to this one. "People in this plant have the 'freedom of choice' in your words, to be represented by an Independent or an International. We can't keep an international out. Employees can join an international whenever they want. If that isn't freedom, I don't know what you mean by freedom."

"And what if they did?" the business agent asked. "You prefer an independent. Would you treat them the same way? No! You wouldn't. That's my point. People have no choice, but to stay with independents."

"Maybe we wouldn't treat people in the same fashion if they belonged to an International," the assistant plant manager returned. "I don't think we would be that different. Maybe we would. But, they still have the freedom of choice."

"But, that is no real choice," the business agent said. "That's like asking a man if he wants to be shot or hung."

The question of "freedom of choice" was kicked around at great length with neither management or the union able to agree. This particular issue got more attention than it deserved. Management and the union seemed to be sparring for the moment—each testing for an opening.

Decentralization another tool. "Decentralization is another anti-International strategy of the company," the business agent said as he shifted the topic. "It spreads us so thin that we can't be effective. That's the strategy behind scattering plants from one end of the country to the next. You say we misinterpret your economic moves; we say that headquarters' real motive is to get rid of International, not just to pinch a few of their pennies they so dearly love."

The union operates democratically. "One of your points that we really can't understand is that 'the union is run by a clique.' Nothing could be further from the truth. We think management has this impression because it doesn't understand how we operate. You have never been to a union meeting. Well, let me change that to say only Joe and Pete, who were once in the union, have been to union meetings. You guys ought to attend one to see what really happens. And you should read our by-laws to learn how we operate. Our organization is more democratic than yours."

The employee relations manager interrupted to say, "What the by-laws say and what really happens can be completely different. Didn't you just recently pass a dues raise when only a minority— the usual 10 per cent—were present? I don't call that representing the total membership."

"I don't know who your stool pigeon is," the union president shot back, "but he sure gave you some bum information."

"This is a good example of how little you know about us," the business manager said. "Let us tell you the procedure. It's in our by-laws.

"In the first place, there is no executive board in the union. Our total membership makes all decisions. They instruct us, the committee, what to do. We couldn't pass a dues raise just because we wanted to. In such instances, a two-thirds majority of those present needs to vote in such a move. If two-thirds doesn't pass it, then the issue has to be brought up by the minority for a revote at the next meeting. It takes three consecutive meetings. Each time such an issue is to come up for a vote, the members are notified a week in advance. They know the time and the place of the meeting. We can't even shift that.

"The committee continually asks for instructions from the floor. For example, we ask the members whether we should take a grievance to the next level. And, we keep people posted on negotiations or anything else important."

Full communications. The business agent continued, "This brings me to another point in your image of us; namely, that we don't communicate with our people. We discuss what is going on with our people in *every* meeting."

Again, the employee relations manager interrupted, "But, when only 10 or 15 per cent is present, not very many people know what is going on. During the recent wage negotiations, your people didn't seem to be well informed on what the real issues were. If they were communicated to, someone was sure editing and censoring what was reported.

"I don't think your people understand the tactics you use. Your continued fixed position in bargaining is not based on the commitment of your people. It's just a tactic of brinkmanship you always use to try to get us to shift our position. When you see we won't be buffaloed, you back off. Your people would never go beyond the brink and strike, particularly when they know the issues."

"At our last meetings during wage negotiations, over 75 per cent of the membership attended," the union president said. "At that time, we reported everything. If we take a position in bargaining, it is because that's what our people want. And, don't be too sure they wouldn't strike if you pushed us into it."

No concern for production. The business agent went to his last point. "You also said we were not interested in production—that we were not concerned with your problems. The truth is, you don't want us to be interested; that is, not beyond the point of doing what management wants. This kills any incentive or concern for management's viewpoint."

"You know what management's attitude is?" the union vice-president asked. "It is, *'Look, you are supposed to do what you are told as you are told. We are not interested in your ideas.'* With that kind of attitude, how can you expect us to act differently? Employees today want to be autonomous and make a real work contribution. And, that doesn't mean through some corny suggestion program."

The employee relations manager, who had been listening intently all this time, stood up with a look of disbelief on his face. He didn't seem to realize he was on his feet. "Do you mean to say you people are *really interested in production?*" He had listened to the union say this for two days, but he had just "heard" it for the first time. His next question was a simple one, but it triggered an hour-long discussion. He asked, "What could management do to use people more effectively?"

A Period of Progress

The earlier period of self-analysis and this exchange made it possible for both to "hear" better what the other was saying. In turn, both sides were able to communicate their attitudes and feelings more openly—more honestly. Some points of agreement and similarities came to the fore as differences were examined, put into perspective, and understood.

Progress was made and better understanding achieved during this latter exchange. Yet under the surface, tensions still remained. Neither side was owning up any more than the other. Old bargaining habits still permeated the exchange. On many points, one side was unable to see why the other felt or thought as it did. Often, members yielded to the temptation to explain why the others were "wrong" in the way they interpreted a situation.

Overall, though, both sides were listening better to each other. Although not always agreeing, they were hearing out each other. As the session continued, questions and replies gained the quality of clarifying rather than of attacking or defending.

The remainder of the day was spent thrashing through the many points of differences that had been uncovered in the early development of images. Both the union and management "ventilated" quite freely. They were thus able to get many things off their chests.

Phase VII: Consolidation of Key Issues

Although far from having talked out their differences, the last part of the day was devoted to identifying those issues which seemed critical in the relationship. Working with the behavioral scientists, union and management jointly identified, as barriers, those issues that would require more examination, discussion and resolution if relations were to be improved. They were summarized as follows.

1. Lack of mutual trust and respect. This was tagged as a key element by both groups. The general feeling was that once genuine trust and respect was achieved, many other things would fall into place. Management's preference for Independents, yet its position that it wanted to learn to work with the International, was cited as an issue that needed better understanding.

2. Ideological differences. Both agreed there existed wide differences in purposes and principles. Common purposes would need to be identified if joint problem-solving was to become a reality. The formulation of this issue, it should be noted, was based on the assumption of both groups that, now, "agreement is possible," had replaced the former notion, "agreement is not possible."

3. Inadequate knowledge and understanding. During the exchanges, it became clear to both sides that many factual matters about each other were not known. Both the union and management felt that neither understood how the other operated—how decisions, regulations, long-range plans, traditions, etc., were handled.

4. Attitudinal differences. Differences in attitudes toward each other, plant operations and the management of business affairs, existed between union and management. Part of this was recognized as a difference in perspective—part was seen as due to different levels of knowledge and to past experiences and relations.

5. Need for more effective use of people. Both agreed there should be more participation and involvement of wage people in the operations of the plant. "We don't want to co-manage," the union said, "but there are some areas where we have high stakes. In these matters, we want to be consulted. We think we can contribute to the effectiveness of operations."

6. Better understanding of rights and obligations. Union and management, they felt, needed to understand better and respect the rights and obligations each has toward the other. There existed a need for better understanding and acceptance of each party's role in the bargaining process. Included was the feeling that each needed a better understanding of the mutual expectations held for the other.

7. Better communications. It was also felt that management and the union needed to communicate more openly, freely, and honestly with each other. Both felt that communication barriers precipitated many of their problems.

8. Better listening. Along with a need for better communications, both sides felt they needed to listen more and better to the other. For example, the union pointed out that employees were concerned with and wanted their views heard on the economic health of the plant. One union member remarked, "I know right now how to save the plant $10,000, but I haven't found anyone that will listen to me. I gave up trying a long time ago."

Planning Next Steps

The final period was devoted to debating what followup steps, if any, should be taken. It was agreed that many tensions and a residue of hostility still existed. Much remained to be talked out before the two sides would be able to work together in an effective manner.

The two groups decided to spend some time considering what they had learned during the laboratory. Both wanted to discuss the results and consider the next best step. Each wanted to report to its members the progress made, to get their reactions, and then to make a tentative proposal of what they felt should be done next. With this, the Union-Management Laboratory ended.

SUMMARY

Several key features of the prevailing relationship between the International and management prior to the laboratory merit a brief consideration by way of summary. These features can be regarded as some of the major barriers that repeatedly emerged during the two days of the laboratory. To a large extent, they remained as issues needing more thrashing out in order to achieve any real degree of understanding.

From the union's standpoint. The union showed great concern for and tested, throughout the two days, the local autonomy of management. There was considerable anxiety over what they saw as corporate ideology and implementation of an anti-International objective. The real question to the union, although they were not able to focus on it, was not whether management had local autonomy, but the *degree* of autonomy management had.

The union was convinced that management was ''dollar-oriented" all the way, without values with respect to people. Therefore, the union felt bound to counteract this "inhumanity" they saw in management.

Management's perspective. Management again and again, demonstrated extreme suspicion of the anti-democracy of the union and the "clique" of union leadership. Management genuinely felt that the union leaders did not represent the people.

Management's attitude was that the union was an institution with intrinsic goals of protecting and building itself. Management felt strongly on two points: (1) that the union had no concern for productivity and (2) that it only had an administrative concern for people, *i.e.*, wage rates, seniority, class and scope of work, security, etc. In other words, management saw the union's concern for people to be an institutional one—that is its business—not a genuine interest in people.

Similarities not seen. Several points of similarity were not observed by either management or the union because of their concern for the *differences* between them. For example, management saw itself as *production-oriented*. The union also saw this. But, management also had a *human* interest which the union did not recognize.

On the other hand, the union saw itself as having a *people* obligation. This, in turn, management recognized in the union. The disparity here was that management did not see the same weight being attached to productivity by the union.

What the two groups, the International and management, shared in common, then, they were not able to recognize. More importantly, what they shared in *common* they saw as *differences*. Under these conditions, disagreement was inevitable, and agreement was impossible. Only by a strategy which held up for examination these deep lying attitudes, was it possible to discover areas of common stake. These, then could serve as the basis for an altered set of assumptions—"disagreement is not inevitable; agreement is possible."

CONCLUSIONS

Intergroup conflict undergirds much of modern, complex organization life. More than ever there is greater interdependence between the groups. This interdependence can help move organizations toward the accomplishment of mutual goals, or, it can breed

hostile and disruptive conflicts. Once conflict erupts, it is difficult to control. It can consume everything and everyone it touches.

The Intergroup Laboratory permits those groups in conflict to
come together and work through the tensions and frictions that
have built up during extended hostility. Confrontation at this level
permits participants to get beneath the issues separating them and
to gain knowledge of the misunderstandings and associated tensions.
Once areas of friction have been identified and tensions reduced,
the two groups can effectively solve their operational problems.

It should be emphasized, however, that an intervention of this
magnitude does not occur in a vacuum. Rather, it takes place within
a stream of day-to-day feeling and issues. For this reason, one
should not expect that a single confrontation, such as just described,
will repeal all present positions, past practices, previous agreements,
etc. It is unlikely such conditions will be greatly influenced, if at all.

Where the greatest impact will become evident, is when *new* issues
and different problems arise. Here, the parties are able to apply
themselves in a problem-solving manner. In other words, the background of conflict does not recede. Rather, it remains to color and
influence old issues born in that era. However, new issues, that do
not have a past anchorage, do not have the same tug in the directions of old norms and past practices. Members in both groups are
not bound by old expectations. Instead, they are free to explore
jointly for new solutions under the collaborative conditions produced by the intergroup therapy sequence.

One other point deserves special emphasis. Correcting a situation
of long-term, chronic hostility requires continuous and diligent
followup efforts. As much as a five-year span may be needed before
the root system that produced the original animosities can be replaced by a new and healthier root system—one that can cause the
relationship to flourish.

References

1. Blake, R. R. and Mouton, J. S. "The Intergroup Dynamics of Win-
Lose Conflict and Problem-Solving Collaboration in Union-Management
Relations," In M. Sherif (Ed.), *Intergroup Relations and Leadership*.
New York: Wiley, 1962, 94-140; and Blake, R. R. and Mouton, J. S.

"Union-Management Relations: From Conflict to Collaboration." *Personnel*, 38, 1961. Blake, R. R. and Mouton, J. S. Intergroup Therapy. *Int. J. of Soc. Psychiat.* 8, (3), 1963, 196-198.

2. Blake, R. R. and Mouton, J. S. *The Managerial Grid.* Houston: Gulf Publishing Co., 1964, Chapter 12.

3. For a review of relevant experimental work, see Blake, R. R. and Mouton, J. S. "Overevaluation of Own Group's Product in Intergroup Competition." *J. of Abnorm. and Soc. Psychol.*, 64, (3), 1962, 237-238; Blake, R. R. and Mouton, J. S. "Comprehension of Points of Communality in Competing Solutions." *Sociometry*, 25, (1), 1962, 56-63; Blake, R. R. and Mouton, J. S. "Comprehension of Own and Outgroup Positions Under Intergroup Competition." *J. of Confl. Resolut.*, 5, (3), 1961, 304-310; Blake R. R. and Mouton, J. S. "Loyalty of Representatives to Ingroup Position during Intergroup Competition." *Sociometry*, 24, (2), 1961, 171-183; Blake, R. R. and Mouton, J. S. "Preceived Characteristics of Elected Representatives." *J. of Abnorm. and Soc. Psychol.*, 62, (3), 1961, 693-695; and, Blake, R. R. and Mouton, J. S. "Reactions to Intergroup Competition Under Win-Lose Conditions." *Mgmt. Sci* 7, (4), 1961, 420-425. Blake, R. R. and Mouton, J. S., *Group Dynamics—Key to Decision Making.* Houston: Gulf Publishing Co., 1961.

Also, for a review and discussion of the prototype intergroup experiments, see Sherif, M., Harvey, O. J., White, B. J., Hood, W. R. and Sherif, C. W. *Intergroup Conflict and Cooperation. The Robbers Cave Experiment.* Institute of Group Relations; Norman, Oklahoma, 1961; Sherif, M. "Superordinate Goals in the Reduction of Intergroup Conflict." *American Journal of Sociology*, 43, 1958, 349-356; Sherif, M. and Sherif, C. *Outline of Social Psychology* (Rev. Ed.), New York: Harper, 1956; and, Sherif, M. and Sherif, C. *Groups in Harmony and Tension.* New York: Harper, 1953.

Author Index

A

Arensberg, C. H., 16
Auigdor, R., 48

B

Bass, B. M., 16
Beckhard, R., 113
Blake, R. R., 16, 17, 32, 47, 48, 49,
    57, 62, 75, 85, 100, 112, 113, 121,
    145, 152, 155, 194, 195
Blanchard, R. E., 112
Blansfield, M. G., 152
Boulding, K. E., 49, 85

C

Cartwright, D., 16
Chalmers, W. E., 31
Cohery, A. R., 17
Coleman, J. R., 85
Cooper, E., 33
Cooper, H. C., 17
Coser, L. A., 57
Crook, W. H., 48

D

Dalton, M., 48
Das, V. P., 33
Dashiell, V. F., 32
Dearden, J., 49
Decatur, S., 27
Derber, M., 31
Deutsch, M., 32, 33
Diesing, P., 85
Doherty, R. P., 47
Douglas, A., 112
Drewes, D. W., 112
Dubin, R., 47

E-F

Edelman, M., 31
Evan, W. M., 112
Faris, R. E. L., 16
Flint, A. W., 16

G

Garfield, S., 85
Gerard, H. B., 16
Goffman, E., 33
Goldman, M., 32
Gotterer, M., 46
Grossack, M. M., 32

H

Haire, M., 49
Hamblin, R. L., 16, 32
Hammond, L. K., 32
Harbison, F. H., 85
Hartman, P. T., 32, 48
Harvey, O. J., 32, 33, 62, 195
Hewlett, Allen, 32
Hood, W. R., 32, 62, 195
Hurlock, E. B., 32

J-K

Jahoda, M., 33
Jones, E. E., 47
Katy, D., 100
Kelley, H. H., 16, 17
Kerr, C., 112
Kunarngo, R., 33

L

Landsberger, H. A., 57
Lansburgh, R. H., 17
Litwak, E., 49
Lundberg, G. A., 112

M-N

McMurray, R., 47
McPherson, W. H., 112
Maller, V. G., 32
Mangum, G. L., 48
March, V. G., 49
Meyer, A. S., 112
Miller, F. G., 47
Miller, K., 16
Mouton, J. S., 17, 32, 33, 47, 48, 49,
    57, 62, 75, 85, 100, 112, 113, 121,
    145, 152, 155, 194, 195
Muench, G. A., 48, 113, 145
Newman, L. E., 85

P

Petro, S., 31
Phipps, T. E., Jr., 62
Pryer, M. W., 16

R

Remmers, H. H., 47
Remmers, L. J., 47
Rohrer, J. H., 16
Ross, A. M., 32, 48
Roy, D., 100

Subject Index